Otunba Jide Omiyale – The Dropship Entrepreneur.

Otunba Jide Omiyale – The Dropship Entrepreneur.

Copyright 2024

Without the author's specific permission, we do not anticipate any portion of this book being copied or communicated in any way, including electronically, by photocopy, or by any information storage system.

However, reviewers are free to use excerpts from the work in their articles in newspapers and publications.

Otunba Jide Omiyale (MBA, FCIM)

Dedication.

This book is dedicated to all persons striving to make the world a better place. Those who want to leave the word better than they met it.

Acknowledgement.

We acknowledge the assistance of https://www.freeimages.com/ And Google creative for the images used in this work. Also U.S. Custom and boarder protection and Nigeria sites for list of Prohibited and restricted items

Special Notice.

It's possible for readers to notice that this book has both British and American spellings.

Readers might, for instance, notice color in certain places and color in others.

We humbly ask for your compassion in accepting both British and American spellings as being accurate.

Acceptance of Responsibility.

We do not lay claim to any perfection, nobody is. Consequently, we accept full responsibility for any deficiency readers might find in this work. We will cheerfully receive any suggestion to improve on this.

Legal Notice.

While we have made all attempts to verify the information provided in this publication, neither the author nor the publisher assumes any responsibility for errors, omissions, or contrary interpretations of the materials here in this book.

The materials herein may be subject to varying state and/or local, and indeed, federal laws and regulations.

Before you commit resources to any project in this book, confirm the regulations guiding such investments from the local government level to the federal level.

Federal, state, and local government professional licensing, business practices, advertising, and all other aspects of doing business in the country are the sole responsibility of the purchaser or reader.

The author and publisher assume no responsibility or liability whatsoever on behalf of any purchaser or reader of this material.

This is material that any person can follow and be successful in business. Your success depends on your commitment.

Any perceived slights against specific individuals, professionals, races, or organizations are unintentional

Otunba Jide Omiyale – The Dropship Entrepreneur.

Contents

Copyright 2024 2
Dedication. 2
Acknowledgement. 2
Special Notice. 2
Acceptance of Responsibility. 3
Legal Notice. 3
Chapter 1: Introduction. 11
Chapter 2: What Is Dropshipping? 14
    Why Should You Do Dropshipping? 15
    Why Droshipping Is Better Than Affiliate Marketing? 16
    Is It All Roses For Dropshippers Then? 17
    Three Biggest Problems Of Dropshippers. 18
    Types of Dropshipping Business Models................ 19
Chapter 3: How To Choose A Dropshipping Niche And Product? 21
Chapter 4: Manufacturers Or Suppliers, Which Way For The Dropshipper? 25
    Supplier's Red Flags... 27
    What To Look For In A Manufacturer...................... 28
    Manufacturer Red Flag. 29
Chapter 5: Searching For Suppliers. 30
    Almighty Google. You will be tempted to go to Google for your dropshippers like many will do and I trust Google will not disappoint you, as it will return loads of pages. 30

Otunba Jide Omiyale – The Dropship Entrepreneur.

Attending Trade Shows. 30

Ask Colleagues: 31

Competition Check. 31

Chapter 6: The Top Dropshippers' Suppliers. 32

AliExpress. https://www.AliExpress.com/ 32

Alibaba: https://www.alibaba.com/ 33

Salehoo: https://www.salehoo.com/ 33

Oberlo: https://www.oberlo.com/ 33

Worldwide Brands: https://www.worldwidebrands.com/
.... 34

Doba: https://www.doba.com/ 34

SunriseWholesale:
https://www.sunrisewholesalemerchandise.com/ 34

Wholesale Central.
https://www.wholesalecentral.com/index.htm. 35

Megagoods. https://www.megagoods.com/index.php. ... 35

Wholesale2B: https://www.wholesale2b.com/index.html
.... 35

Printful: https://www.printful.com/ 35

Chapter 7: Choosing The Best Supplier For Your
Dropshipping Business. 37

Age and Experience. 37

Are Fees Legitimate? 38

How Fast Their Shipping Is: 39

Product Quality. 39

Customer Service. 39

Suitable Return Policy: 39

Otunba Jide Omiyale – The Dropship Entrepreneur.

Location Of Your Supplier And Market. 40

Competition Check. 40

Contacting Your Supplier. 41

A Contact Letter Template. 42

Chapter 8: Starting A Dropshipping Store? 44

Setting Up Your Own Website. 44

Advantages Of Having Your Own Site. 45

Factors To consider when Choosing An Ecommerce Platform. 46

Chapter 9: The Best 5 Ecommerce Platforms To Boost Your Dropshipping. 50

Bottom Line. 54

Chapter 10: Building You Dropshipping Store And See Your Products Zoom Off The Digital Shelve. 55

Chapter 11: Proven Marketing Tactics For Dropshippers. 58

1. Facebook, Instagram, Google, and TikTok Ads. 59

2. TikTok Marketing And IG Reels Can Make You Go Viral. 60

3. Email Marketing. 62

4. Blog. 64

6. Add Reviews Of Your Product On Your Site. 65

7. Concise And Catchy Descriptions: 66

8. Easy Checkout Flow. 66

9. Influencers, You Heard About Them? 67

10. Use Brand Ambassadors And Affiliates. 68

11. YouTube Channel, You Need It. 68

12. Recover Abandoned Carts. 69

13. You Have To Upsell And Cross Sell. ... 70
14. Join Your Digital Communities. ... 71
15. Promotions, Competitions And Giveaway. ... 71
16. Get Good Product Photograph. ... 72
17. User Generated Content Works Like Magic. ... 73
18. Conclusion. ... 74

Chapter 12: Beginners Mistakes In Dropshipping. ... 75
1. Too High Expectations: ... 75
2. Too Much Research. ... 76
3. Inadequate Product Research. ... 77
4. Covering Too Much Ground. ... 78
5. Choosing The Wrong Niche. ... 78
6. Supplier's Reliability. ... 79
7. Putting Too Much Trust On A Supplier. ... 79
8. Price Undercutting. ... 79
9. Neglecting Customer Reviews And Feedback: ... 80
10. No Optimized Website: ... 81
11. No Marketing Plan. ... 81
12. Using Unethical SEO Practices (Black Hat). ... 82
13. Using Influencers: ... 82
14. No Established System For Returns. ... 83
15. Inadequate Financial Planning and Monitoring: ... 83
16. Disregarding Tax and Legal Responsibilities ... 83
17. Not Taking Holidays Into Consideration. ... 84
18. Dropping Off Early. ... 84

Chapter 13: Prohibited and Restricted Items. ... 85

The USA. 86

Nigeria. 87

Chapter 14: How To Register Your Business. 90

Choosing Your Business Name: 90

Company Structure. 90

Registering Your Business Name. 91

Employer Identification Number (EIN): 91

Chapter 15: Dropshipping With Amazon 94

Advantages Of Amazon Dropshipping. 95

Disadvantages of Amazon Dropshipping. 95

Steps To Starting Dropshipping In Amazon. 95

Amazon Dropshipping And Amazon FBA. 96

Conclusion 96

Chapter 16: Important KPIs For Tracking Dropshipping Profitability 97

What are Key Performance Indicators (KPI)? 97

What Role Does KPI Play In Your Dropshipping Success? 98

Sales Revenue. 98

Average Order Value. 99

Calculating Customer Lifetime Value (CLV Or LTV) 99

Monitoring Conversion Rate. 100

Customer Acquisition Cost (CAC) 100

Cost Per Lead. 101

The total cost to get a prospective customer by providing their email or phone number is called the cost per lead. This is usually obtained when you entice a customer with a gift for their contact information. (See email marketing) 101

Cart Abandonment Rate. 101

Gross Profit Margin Indicator. 102

Conclusion. 102

Chapter 17: A Dropshipping Case Study. 103

Getting A Niche And Product. 103

1.Amazon.   https://www.amazon.com/gp/bestsellers
.... 104

2.Lightinthehouse.
http://www.lightinthebox.com/c/best-sellers-511_72965
.... 106

.... 106

3.Temu.   https://www.temu.com/channel/best-sellers.html? 107

4.AliExpress
https://www.AliExpress.com/w/wholesale-top-ranking-products.html?spm=a2g0o.home.history.2.650c76dbF2LjQu 107

5.Etsy https://www.etsy.com/market/best_selling_items
.... 108

.... 108

Validation. 108

Social Media Validation 109

#1. Instagram 109

#2: Facebook 109

#3.Twitter (X) 110

Conclusion. 111

Otunba Jide Omiyale – The Dropship Entrepreneur.

Coming Up With a Name and a Logo. 111

Building The Store. 113

Payment Gateway. 115

Description. 115

Marketing. 116

Email 117

Facebook. 117

Blogging. 118

Pricing. 118

Tools For Dropshipping. 119

Write A Review 120

About The Author. 120

Chapter 1: Introduction.

Thanks to the internet, there are now many business models people can use to make money from the comfort of their homes.

Many do internet business to support their 9-5 hustles to settle bills and live a better life.

Among the ways to make money from the internet are blogging, writing as authors and selling on KDP, or just being a ghostwriter for other authors.

You can do FBA on Amazon, affiliate marketing with Click Bank and other marketplaces, or register with Fiver to render your skills to customers for a fee, and here the opportunities are endless.

There is hardly any skill you cannot market on Fiver, graphic design, video making, content creation, advertising, and so many others.

And then you have YouTube, with its own business opportunities to harvest from.

Indeed, the internet has opened up the business world to allow all of us to have a bite.

One of the profitable businesses you can do without leaving the corners of your home on the internet is dropshipping. A business you do with only your computer and data with no significant capital outlay.

It's a lazy man's way to riches. You can build a six-figure business empire with this model. It is the ultimate business strategy that enables you to sell huge stocks without lifting a finger.

Oh, except on your laptop.

Therefore, why isn't dropshipping already being used by everyone?

Why do so many people still prefer to become affiliate marketers in order to generate income?

The explanation is straightforward: many individuals are still unaware of what dropshipping is or how to get involved in it. Naturally, this book will change all of that by educating you on dropshipping's definition, advantages, and how to get started.

By the end, you will be operating your own dropshipping company and earning money from sales of goods branded with your logo without any up-front costs or financial risks.

Read about the advantages of dropshipping over affiliate marketing later.

But first, this:

When I was writing, *'How To Import From China'*, now and then, I got drifted to Dropshipping territory, and it dawned on me that I would need to write on dropshipping because it is easy to equate simple importation with dropshipping.

Simple importation may look like dropshipping, but they are not the same.

Otunba Jide Omiyale – The Dropship Entrepreneur.

Ordinary importation is self- and personal purchases you make and probably sell off a few products to friends, family members, church members, and neighbors, while dropshipping is a business model you can use to make loads of money.

Unlike simple personal importation, you need some special skills to survive in the dropshipping space, hence the birth of 'The Dropship Entrepreneur'.

The ideal business plan is one that lets you sell large stocks without having to do much work.

Chapter 2: What Is Dropshipping?

Dropshipping is a business model where you get a customer to pay for a product you sell and you send the payment to your supplier at an agreed price and your supplier sends the product to your customer and you keeping the difference between the cost price from your supplier and the price paid by your customer.

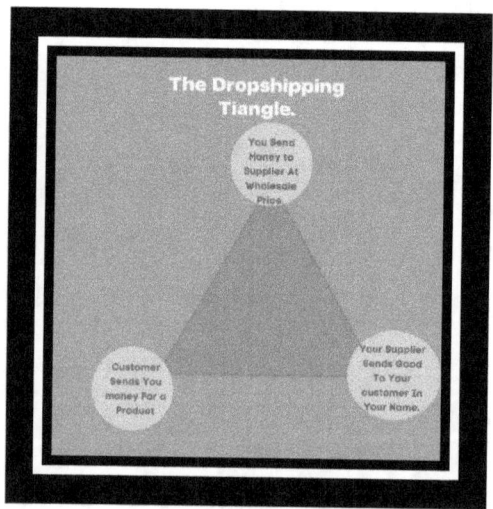

Clearly, you now see the difference between mere importation and dropshipping. It will occur to you that you will need a supplier to sell to you in bulk and you must have a customer to buy the product.

Among others, you will need the skill to find the right product to sell, you will need to find where to get these products, and you will also need to find the customer to buy, besides all the intricacies of business involved.

Otunba Jide Omiyale – The Dropship Entrepreneur.

Can you make money from dropshipping? Yes, you can, if done properly, following the tips in this book. But I must warn, it is not a million-dollar-overnight-business.

Like all genuine businesses, it needs hard work, consistency, and commitment. There are thousands all over the world doing good for themselves with this model.

The secret is to niche down and promote. Niche down means find a product with little completion and promote.

Why Should You Do Dropshipping?

These are what attract people to dropshipping as a business model

- Ease Of Starting. It is easy to start, even if you are green in internet business. All you need to do is to find an irresistible product and buyers.
- Low Capital: Unlike many other businesses where you have to hold inventory, Dropshipping does not require that. The biggest starting outlay may be the cost of hosting your site, which may be as little as $20 a month.
- Large Products Base to Choose From. You have a huge stock of products from many suppliers to choose from.
- Little or No Overhead. As you don't carry inventory or a physical office, there is little or no overhead for you to carry. You can work without a secretary and messenger; at least in the initial stage, it's you and your laptop with data.
- Little Or No Risk. There is absolutely no risk because you carry no inventory. Collect the customer's money, send it to your supplier. However, be honest, because

> you will eventually get into hot water if you game the system.
> ➢ No Physical Location Necessary. You don't carry an inventory, so there is no need to keep a warehouse for goods at extra cost.
> ➢ Easy To Upscale. Simply put, you do the same work for 5 orders as one order. On the other hand, with average retailer, they have to work five times as one to execute five orders. The packaging, handling, etc. become the supplier's problems.

Why Droshipping Is Better Than Affiliate Marketing?

Although this sounds a lot like affiliate marketing, there are a few important distinctions.

To begin with, you will typically make more money than through affiliate marketing. Resellers typically use a pricing strategy known as "keystone pricing."

Keystone pricing indicates that you are charging twice as much for the product as you are paying the manufacturers. This is one of the most widely followed practices for this kind of business, and dropshipping companies are essentially resellers.

Dropshipping has one major advantage over affiliate marketing, which is the absence of a need to publicly announce the presence of the supplier.

Stated differently, the buyer is unaware that someone else is marketing the item. You're just selling them the stuff as though it were your own and not directing them to another website where they can check out and buy it later.

Otunba Jide Omiyale – The Dropship Entrepreneur.

This is great news since it makes your company appear much more professional and eliminates the need to drive customers away from your brand in order to increase sales.

In affiliate marketing, the buyer sees you as a middleman, but in dropshipping, he sees you as a complete one-stop entity even as you sell another person's product.

Is It All Roses For Dropshippers Then?

No, it's not. There are disadvantages in dropshipping like any other business.

Here are what dropshippers should know.

- ➤ Low profit margin. Compared to retailers, dropshippers make lower margins. But that may not be completely true, there are instances where you can make 100% profit on some products, such as electronics, for example. It depends, and this is where the acquired skill comes in handy.
- ➤ Competition. There are many dropshippers out there because of the ease of entry into the business, but you can overcome that by narrowing it down to specifics. E.g., hearing aids for grandmas.
- ➤ Difficulty In Inventory Management. Because you do not have direct knowledge of your supplier's inventory, sometimes it's difficult to manage inventory on your side. You may place orders for products that are out of stock, which may result in problems with your own customers, necessitating continuous dialogue with your suppliers. You may also lose track of orders if there's no close rapport with your supplier.
- ➤ Complexities in Shipping. This is expected. For example, if your customer orders four unique items

Otunba Jide Omiyale – The Dropship Entrepreneur.

from four different companies, it means you pay four different shipping costs, which lowers your margin.

Fortunately, these days, you may get over this by working with few suppliers with large and diverse inventory for your customer to choose from. Niche down your suppliers.

- ➢ You Are Responsible For Your Suppliers Error. If your supplier errs, it's on you. Your customer knows you, deals with you, not your supplier, and that's why you must choose suppliers wisely.
- ➢ You Cannot Brand. Since your supplier sends straight to your customer, you have no control over the brand. And unless you have a way of doings some promotions on your side to your customers, you cannot do it with the packaging. However, there are suppliers who are ready to brand for you if you ask.

Three Biggest Problems Of Dropshippers.

Having established what dropshipping is, as a price arbitrage where you find a product at a cheap price, sell at a higher price and keep the margin, it is pertinent to discuss the problems a dropshipper will have to overcome to have a successful business.

There are three major challenges, and we will espouse on each.

1. Getting A Product To Sell. Getting a profitable product to sell may very well be the biggest problem for a droppshipper. It is not that there is a scarcity of product to sell, on the contrary, there are millions, but choosing the right one is the problem. Dropshippers have to choose right here.

Otunba Jide Omiyale – The Dropship Entrepreneur.

2. Getting A Reliable Supplier: This too could be a big problem as a wobble supplier can ruin your business. You don't know them, you may not have visited them as you only rely on information provided and all errors they make along the line bounce back on you.

Again, you have to choose wisely. Your supplier could be a manufacturer you are dealing with directly or enormous stores like 1688 or AliExpress. As we progress, we will discuss the pros and cons of each.

3. Getting The Buyers. How do you get the buyers is another challenge. You may have the best product in the world, but without buyers, you won't make a dime.

Here, marketing comes in. Are you having a site of your own or using a built platform like Shopify, eBay or Amazon?

Are you using Facebook or Instagram to advertise? Are you blogging? We will get to address those issues later.

But now, what are the types of dropshipping possible?

Types of Dropshipping Business Models.

1. **Product Reselling:** This is the commonest form of dropshipping where you have most people. In fact, most dropshippers started from here. It involves finding a product, listing it on your site and getting customers to buy. You send the money to your supplier, who in turn sends the good to your customer under your name.
2. **Print on Demand:** Here you have designs you send to your suppliers to print on products to sell to your customers. You can print on textiles like T-shirts, on mugs and even writing materials for schools. It's

endless. This is a model for politicians and churches where there is a large membership.
3. **Labeling:** This should be the ultimate aim of a dropshipper especially when you have a product that is popular. You ask your supplier to brand the product with your brand name. This gives your product a unique brand. In offline business, people do this. For example, oil companies can brand engine oil for you.
4. **Reverse Dropshipping:** You reverse dropshipping, selling to a normally exporting country from an importing country. For example, importing from the USA to China

Chapter 3: How To Choose A Dropshipping Niche And Product?

We have stated that you need to find a profitable product to sell, but how do you get that product without first finding a niche?

A niche is a segment of the market.

For example, automobile is a market, but here you have niches like cars, trucks and so on. And under cars, you have sub-niche, like saloon cars and sedan cars. Under saloon cars, you can branch to brands like Toyotas and even niche down further to Toyota Corolla. You get the gist, narrowing down the niche to get to a specific one.

Alright, you are not selling cars; I'll give you examples in consumables.

Let us do a niche down on men's watches. You have the general watch, then you have a military watch, led watch, gold watch and wooden watch. You have for men, women and kids. So you can niche down to boy's watches or men's wooden watches.

Yet another example. Under bags, you have man's bags, woman's bags, travel bags, luxury bags, cross bags and so on. You can niche down to women luxury bags and may even niche down to brands of luxury bags. Ladies Gucci bags or

Otunba Jide Omiyale – The Dropship Entrepreneur.

women designer handbags without mentioning Gucci. You get the gist. Women's Gucci bags is narrower than Ladies designer bags. Right?

There are two things important about choosing a niche. First, it must be the one you have a feel and passion for, because you cannot sell in a market you do not understand.

If you have a niche you have a passion for, is it evergreen?

Evergreen products are products that sell well throughout the year, not changing with fad or seasons.

They sell whether you are in spring, winter, or summer. An umbrella or rain boot, no matter how beautiful, will sell well only in rainy season.

This takes us to the difference between an evergreen product and a product that trends

A trending product sells well for a period because it's popular and people are asking for them. With time, the sale falls. You may take advantage of a trending product, but you cannot build a lasting business on them.

You need a product that sells year in, year out.

Phone accessories, gaming products, and beauty products are some examples of evergreen niches.

That a niche is evergreen does not mean you will make good money there, as many people believe. You will face an uphill task to make money if the field is saturated, especially with big players.

Let us cap it up.

Otunba Jide Omiyale – The Dropship Entrepreneur.

Step 1: Begin With Your Passion And Interest. If you are not interested in dogs, don't deal in dog training.

Step 2. Your Own Solved Problem. If you have had a nagging problem solved by a product, you may have stumbled on gold.

Chances are that there are people suffering from that problem and who are in a better position to sell to them than a person who has had the problem and got it solved. You can tell them, hi, I had the issue for five years and this is how I overcame it. Word-of-mouth recommendation.

Step 3. Competition. You will need to research the competition. How competitive is the niche, who are the players, and how much is spent on it?

That a niche is competitive does not mean you cannot take a bite. It is big enough for more. If niche is not competitive and nobody is spending money there, building a dropshipping business on that is a waste of resources.

How do you know products that sell?

You can reach these sites for the best products you can do dropshipping on.

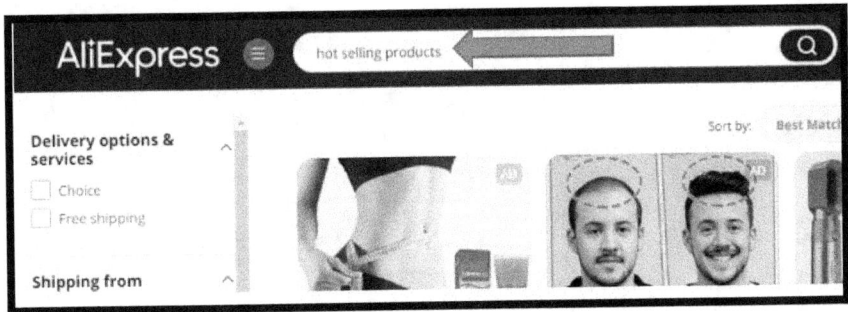

> ➢ AliExpress top selling products.

Otunba Jide Omiyale – The Dropship Entrepreneur.

- Amazon best sellers
- Google trends.
- Titok Hashtags'
- Ebay Trends

As of now, 2024, these are 10 hot niches.
1. **Gaming headset**
2. **Bluetooth speaker**
3. **Smart watches**
4. **Wooden watches**
5. **Teeth whitening kit**
6. **Hair growth serum**
7. **USB charging dock**
8. **Baby carrier**
9. **Smoothie blender**
10. **Organic tea**

You can see they are all evergreen. We will all be having babies. Bald people want more hair and people always want their teeth whiter.

If you search on a big site like AliExpress and you find out a product has many orders, or similar products keep showing up, this may be a sign that the product is moving but then you must answer whether it is an evergreen or just trending.

Chapter 4: Manufacturers Or Suppliers, Which Way For The Dropshipper?

Now you have chosen a product to import and want to decide where to get your product from.

One thing is certain, the source of the product's supplier is very crucial to your business success.

Your reputation with the customer is primarily influenced by the efficiency of your supplier, as they interact with you, assuming you are the supplier.

If your supplier screws up along the line, it's all on you, and you are going to bear the brunt.

There are two choices you have here: to get your product from a supplier or a manufacturer.

A manufacturer manufactures the products, while the supplier gets the products from the manufacturer. However, some manufacturers do agree to sell the products on your behalf, acting as both a manufacturer and a supplier.

One thing that will hit your mind is that getting the product directly from the manufacturer will bring the product to your customer at a lower cost, thereby increasing your margin, but it's not as simple as that.

For some reasons, you may decide to go the supplier route if it means better business.

So, which way?

Otunba Jide Omiyale – The Dropship Entrepreneur.

There are some qualities you need in either a supplier or manufacturer.

1. Super Salespeople: Their sales representatives must be top-notch with expert knowledge of their product and good communication skill and must be warm, not the cold, snobbish type. They may not answer all your questions immediately but must provide answers in a reasonable time.

2. Shipping Time: Your supplier must be able to ship almost immediately, usually within 24 hours and at most within 48 hours. AliExpress and Temu ship within hours. If your supplier takes days to ship, it will harm your business. If your trial order shows they are slow at shipping, dump them and find another source, as the competition in the industry does not allow that.

3. Per-Order Fees. Most suppliers will charge per-order fees, which is understandable as they will expend resources to prepare your order, but the fees should not be killing. You do the calculations, and be sure it leaves enough for you. Usually, it's between $2 and $10.however, some don't charge per-order fees.

4. Quality Products: There is no alternative to this. You must get quality products for your customers to satisfy them so you too can get excellent reviews and more word-of-mouth recommendation and referrals, which will result in more sales. Do not compromise this because of low price, as it will backfire with time. You have to ensure that they meet your quality standard.

5. Technology: Is your supplier up to date in technology? You know if they are investing in technology by the quality of their website and what you can accomplish on it. Can you review orders on the site or get questions asked by a simple email? Is the site static with no new innovations and what of their database? Is it up-to-date and accessible?'

6. Branding. While branding of products ordered at the beginning may not be necessary, the ultimate goal is to be big enough to ask for product branding. Can your supplier accommodate this?

7. Financial Stability: They should be financially stable and not at risk of closing down anytime. During my early days, I dealt with a supplier that I believed was good since they fulfilled all the above criteria, but I was unaware that they were experiencing financial stress. Suddenly they disappeared from the net but I was lucky, I wasn't placing big orders.

8. Industry rating: What are the players in the industry saying about the supplier? Word-of-mouth recommendations are the best form of advertising.

Ultimately, your supplier may not have all these qualities, but you examine the mix and decide. For example, if they cannot brand for you now, they too are trying to be bigger and will brand for you in the future. However, do not compromise on quality and immediate shipping.

Supplier's Red Flags.

When you see these signs from your supplier, you may want to review your doing business with them

1. Shabby shipping time. That is taking over 48 hours to ship.

2. Product quality declining. If the quality of their products is declining, have a rethink.

3. Difficulty In Reaching Them And Taking A Long Time To Reply To Queries. Serious businesses answer promptly and at the latest within 24hours. Amazon does not take up to 24 hours to answer your question. And that is an octopus, so smaller businesses should find a way of responding promptly.

4. Late Deliveries. Prompt delivery is inevitable in this business. So if a supplier keeps delivering late, change them.

5. Tardiness In Sharing Information: They should have nothing to hide in sharing financial, lead-time and delivery schedule information with you. If they are reluctant to do this, you watch it.

What To Look For In A Manufacturer.

- ✓ They must have the capacity to produce your products.
- ✓ They must be able to maintain quality across the board
- ✓ Are other industries players vouching for them? Again, word-of-mouth recommendation.
- ✓ Communicating with them must be easy. Many Chinese reps cannot communicate fluently in English, and some among them have polyglot reps. Communication is important, so you understand one another. Poor communication may lead to the wrong description of a product. Both sides must be sure of what you are talking about.
- ✓ Their price must be competitive. Of course, if they are not, you won't be able to survive among other dropshippers dealing with similar products.
- ✓ They are not to be rigid and dogmatic. Flexibility is the word for customized orders or payment terms

Otunba Jide Omiyale – The Dropship Entrepreneur.

Manufacturer Red Flag.

Check for these red flags.

1. If their quality certification is not up to date

2. If they are reluctant to share information on matters like cost of materials

3. Difficulties when trying to communicate with them. Ignoring emails and things like that.

4. Asking for upfront payment is definitely not the best.

5. Lack of flexibility is also a bad sign. If one of their raw material suppliers fails, they should be able to switch to an alternative immediately.

6. If there is no dedicated point of contact where you can communicate with your team, there will be problems.

Chapter 5: Searching For Suppliers.

Manufactures. Once you have settled for your product, one of the easiest ways to find a supplier is to contact the manufacturers. They should be able to give you a list of the wholesalers they deal with, which you can contact.

Most wholesalers carry similar products from many manufacturers, you will quickly find the right supplier. A couple of calls should give you the suitable ones for your product.

Almighty Google. You will be tempted to go to Google for your dropshippers like many will do and I trust Google will not disappoint you, as it will return loads of pages.

Now, where do you go from here, as the best ones may not have time for SEO and may be buried inside the pages? We don't recommend this route.

Elsewhere in this book, we recommend checking the sites on the internet, but that again may not give you all the answers. Yes, many great suppliers like AliExpress have equally magnificent sites, but some quality suppliers do not have sites befitting their services.

Attending Trade Shows.
Some writers do recommend attending trade shows, which is an expert advice because you can see many manufacturers and suppliers together, ask physical representative face-to-face

question, to increase your knowledge of the products and market at the same place.

The snag here is, how many have the time and the means? However, if you are big enough, attending trade shows may be a great idea.

Ask Colleagues:
Sometimes colleagues can give you recommendations. There are still some out there who believe the sky is big enough for all the birds to fly.

Competition Check.
Sometimes you may want to peek at your competition. Find a droppshipper selling the product, order from him, and check the supplier on the back of the parcel. Contact them when you receive the product.

This may be an excellent technique when you find it hard to get a source, probably because the market is small and so no justification for a supplier.

Remember, sometimes a small market with a few players may mean a jackpot.

When choosing a supplier, you cannot ask too many questions. Ask questions, ask more questions, and ask even more questions.

Otunba Jide Omiyale – The Dropship Entrepreneur.

Chapter 6: The Top Dropshippers' Suppliers.

A thorough analysis of every dropshipping provider and company is outside the purview of this book. There is a very long list of them. Rather, we've highlighted ten of the most well-known web directories for dropshipping suppliers.

AliExpress. https://www.AliExpress.com/

AliExpress is the elephant in the house when it comes to global dropshipping. They connect Big E-commerce companies with droppshippers with most of the products sourced from china.

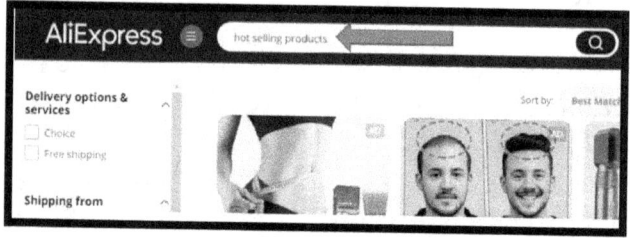

With over a hundred million products covering many categories, such as electronics, fashion, toys, beauty products and even automobiles like motorcycle and cars.

Both green and veteran droppshippers will find AliExpress invaluable as they help in market research, trending products.

It's one stop-shop for dropshippers.

If you want to know about trending products, just go to AliExpress hot products.

Otunba Jide Omiyale – The Dropship Entrepreneur.

Alibaba: https://www.alibaba.com/

Alibaba, the mother of AliExpress, is really a B2B concern linking buyers and sellers together. It's more of a wholesaler than a retailer.

Their shipping may take time—six weeks in some cases for deliveries which make some dropshippers chose to go by air, but you must do your mathematics.

Alibaba is a big one with almost 6000categories of circa 3million products. No wonder they claim to be the leading B2B platform for global trade.

Salehoo: https://www.salehoo.com/

Salehoo is a supplier directory linking you with about 8,000 wholesalers offering dropshipping services, especially those using amazon and eBay platforms.

However, it is a paid service which may not endear to new entrants with little capital. Established dropshippers may find their services handy.

If you have the money, this site may be all you need, as they introduce you to thousands of suppliers which they have vetted. They are also integrated with AliExpress and Shopify.

Oberlo: https://www.oberlo.com/

"Fulfill your dropshipping dream" is how you are welcomed to Oberlo site. With them, you can open an online store with

Otunba Jide Omiyale – The Dropship Entrepreneur.

Shopify without hassles. They manage the shipping, inventory, and packaging.

Oberlo is completely integrated with Shopify e-commerce. You will find out later that many successful dropsippers use Shopify as a hosted platform second only to WooCommerce, which is a self-made by WordPress.

Worldwide Brands:
https://www.worldwidebrands.com/

One of the oldest supplier directories, was founded in 1999. Their list of suppliers is properly vetted to make sure they are legit and meet some standard guidelines. You can use their directory to find niches and reputable wholesalers.

Doba: https://www.doba.com/

Doba automates the order fulfillment process, while linking sellers and suppliers together.

With under 200 suppliers, Doba has a central order base that allows you to place orders with multiple warehouses at the same time.

It is a paid service as well.

SunriseWholesale:
https://www.sunrisewholesalemerchandise.com/

Sunrise Wholesale distributes straight to your consumers and has over 10,000 dropshipping products available. Sunrise also provides product information, email-delivered inventory updates, sales reporting tools, and automated pricing adjustments to guarantee your profit margin stays stable even if suppliers raise or lower their prices.

Otunba Jide Omiyale – The Dropship Entrepreneur.

They ship straight to the USA and Canada.

Wholesale Central.
https://www.wholesalecentral.com/index.htm.

They are different because they do not charge sellers, instead; they charge suppliers who want to be listed in their directory. The site claims to vet all listed suppliers for legitimacy and trustworthiness. They are real dropshippers and real wholesalers.

Megagoods. https://www.megagoods.com/index.php.

Megagoods have a variety of products even though they seem to specialize in consumer electronics. They are wholesalers but still offer dropshipping service, meaning they can ship directly to your customers.

If electronics is where you specialize, then talk to Megagoods.

Wholesale2B:
https://www.wholesale2b.com/index.html

With over a million products, they dropship into your store. The customers pay you, and then you pay wholesale2B. They ship to your customer and you keep the difference operating in UK, Canada and USA from anywhere in the world. A perfect dropshipping platform.

Printful: https://www.printful.com/

As print on demand is an arm of dropshipping model, we have to mention Printful. They specialize in print-on-demand products such as home goods, apparels and accessories. They also ingrate with notable e-commerce platforms.

Otunba Jide Omiyale – The Dropship Entrepreneur.

You create and sell customized products without carrying an inventory. Perfect Dropshipping model.

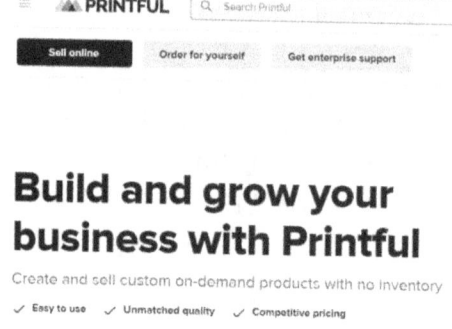

We have dealt with 10 of the prominent suppliers, here are some others.

Cjdropshipping.

CROV.

Spocket.

Modalyst.

Sunrise Wholesale.

Chapter 7: Choosing The Best Supplier For Your Dropshipping Business.

You now have a list of a few of the best suppliers. How do you choose the one that is most suitable for your business?

You may want to access them under the following categories:

Age and Experience.

There is a deluge of suppliers out there, but many are risky, as some are outright dubious and fraudulent. Besides, many rush into this business and rush out.

Therefore, the experience of a supplier in the business is crucial, and so you have to check how long they have been supplying?

If they have been on for 2 years, you may consider them stable.

There are many sites on the internet where you can check the age of a site.

Here are some:

https://smallseotools.com/domain-age-checker/

https://websiteseochecker.com/domain-age-checker/

Otunba Jide Omiyale – The Dropship Entrepreneur.

https://www.whatsmydns.net/domain-age

These are three, you may want to check for more.

AliExpress Age Check With Smallseotools.Com.

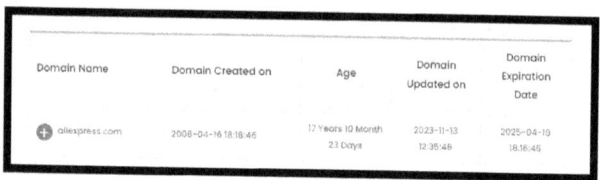

Almost 18 years for AliExpress, no surprise.

This Is Printful Result Using Whatsmydns.Net.

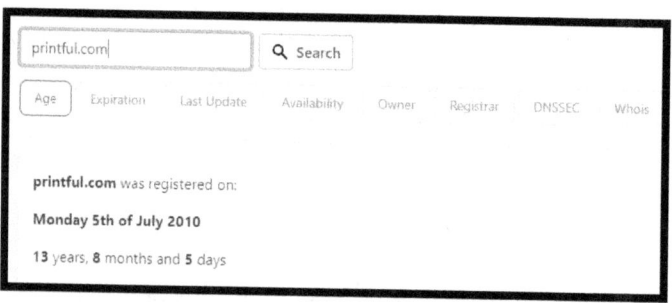

!3 years, 8 months is okay.

Are Fees Legitimate?

As we said elsewhere, it is normal to charge pre-order fees, but you must ask if the fee is legitimate. You will need to do the math and see if there is enough for you.

The industry charge ranges from $2 to $10 to $20.

However, some suppliers do not charge preorder fees, you juggle the information together and make your choice.

How Fast Their Shipping Is:

Shipping must be prompt, preferably within 24 hours. This business has no room for delayed shipping.

Product Quality.

I cannot think of any disadvantage to quality products except a possibly lower margin, but the damage inferior quality products will do to your business is grievous if it does not kill the business.

For quality, there is no compromise.

Customer Service.

Customer service must be top notch. They must answer questions immediately, whether on the phone or by mail. You cannot afford to wait for a response to an inquiry for eternity.

You can test them by sending them an email with a generic question as simple as, what is your minimum order quantity for children's running shoes?

Suitable Return Policy:

In this business, no matter how high the quality of your product is, you will still have returns. So it is imperative for you to know and confirm your supplier's return policy. It must be flexible and suitable enough to make you and your customer happy.

Otunba Jide Omiyale – The Dropship Entrepreneur.

Location Of Your Supplier And Market.

If you can get your supplier from the market where you operate, the better. For example, if your market is in the USA, it's best to source a supplier from the USA for many reasons. You can be fairly sure of the quality and quick shipping time.

But unfortunately, it does not always happen like that. In developing countries like Nigeria, for instance, with little or no manufacturing capacity, you will have to rely on outside suppliers.

Many dropshippers in developing countries depend on suppliers from the east, such as AliExpress. Do your research.

Another reason you may choose a supplier from another region to feed your market is to take advantage of product variation and specialty.

Thus, you can sell in the USA a UK product with different material variations from the USA suppliers and label it as made in Great Britain.

Or if you are selling in a developing country market, you label it USA made, if it is. The perception is that if it's made in the States, it will be of good quality.

Competition Check.

Sometimes you may want to peek at your competition. Find a droppshipper selling the product, order from him, check the supplier on the back of the parcel, and contact them when you receive the product.

Otunba Jide Omiyale – The Dropship Entrepreneur.

This may be an excellent technique when you find it hard to get a source. Probably the market is small and so no justification for a supplier.

Contacting Your Supplier.

You now have a good niche and a great product you want to sell and you have streamlined your prospective suppliers to about three and want to contact them.

Pick The Phone: Contact them on phone and let them be aware you are following up with an email. The way they respond will give you a glimpse of what to expect.

Email. Now follow up with an email asking them relevant questions. Your email should contain the questions you want answered.

The Following Question Need To Be Answered.

Payment Terms: Often, you will get a lower price than the quoted price on the site.

Hidden costs. Are there any other cost besides the price in number one above? You have to be sure of the terms.

Return Policy: Be very clear on this because there will always be unsatisfied customer returning goods.

Do They Sell Direct To Individuals? If the answer is yes, then you will compete with your supplier, which is not good business. It is like an affiliate marketer selling items the product owner is selling directly to users.

Otunba Jide Omiyale – The Dropship Entrepreneur.

Stability Of The Price? How often do they review their prices? You should know of price change well ahead of time to adjust. A sudden price change will affect you negatively.

Expected Gross Profit: This is the selling price minus the cost prices. You get the net profit by deducting other overhead costs.

Yes, you should be able to calculate this yourself, but your supplier should be able to supply this information from experience from other buyers.

Warrantee and Guarantee. You will need to know their policy on this as this will affect the return policy.

Data Feed. Your supplier should have a data feed to allow you to update your store easily.

Custom Built Products. Ultimately, you want to grow to the extent of having your own unique products. Your supplier should be able to do this.

A Contact Letter Template.

Below is a template of a contact letter to a suppler.

Hello,

Having researched on suppliers for my dropshipping product, I have zeroed on your company for supply.

I would like to order soccer training shoes from you and would like you to provide me with information as follows.

> 1. What are your payment terms? Do you charge a preorder fee?

Otunba Jide Omiyale – The Dropship Entrepreneur.

2. What are your return policies as dropshipping is concerned? Here you would like to let me know your guarantee and warrantee policy.

3. What is the percentage of gross profit I could expect from this niche (Soccer training shoes?

4. Do you sell products to individuals apart from bulk buyers for dropshipping?

5. I understand we are operating under a dynamic economic situation, but would be glad to let me know how frequently you change prices and the lead time for dropshippers.

6. With time, I may like to customize my product. Do you have a capacity for such?

Apart from the above, there may be other useful information you may have for dropshippers on this niche. Please oblige me with them. .

Looking forward to mutual fruitful business experience with you

Yours faithfully.

Your name and site if you have one.

You must sound professional, use professional language and no epistles. Nobody has time for that.

Your letter is not likely going to be the first of such with them, so there is the likelihood they shoot you a reply immediately.

Chapter 8: Starting A Dropshipping Store?

You have done your research on suppliers and have ideas of what you want to sell. Maybe you have decided on shoes, consumer electronic, shoes or bags and so on.

The question now is where and how to sell your goods.

There are the two choices open to you and these are.

1. Having your own store on your site built for the dropshipping business.

2. Using one of the established ecommerce hubs

Setting Up Your Own Website.

Owning your own website for droshpping business may be a great idea as you have complete control over your business.

However, for somebody who is not savvy in coding and stuff like that, it may be intimidating.

It is not as bad as that because there are a good deal of software and free site builders like wordless with free themes, you could use but then if you are not an expert in site building it could be a tough assignment and besides, setting up a site for commerce is not the same as setting up a site for blogging.

On the final analysis, you may need a professional to build it for you and you have tons of them on freelance sites like Fiver and Upwork.

Otunba Jide Omiyale – The Dropship Entrepreneur.

Advantages Of Having Your Own Site.

Trustworthiness. Many internet users are still skeptical about buying from some ecommerce giants such as eBay, but if you have a site of your own, it portrays you as a professional, a serious business concern and therefore they trust you more.

No Listing Fees. Fees charged by ecommerce sites eat straight into your profit, which you won't have to pay if you have a site of your own except fees for the payment gateway companies lie PayPal.

Remember you will need to pay for site hosting and the professional to maintain your site and shuffle them around, but happily enough, with time, you yourself may do that.

Eliminate competitors. On ecommerce site like eBay, amazon, there are many competitors competing with you for the same product and you are at a disadvantage if they can get the product at a lower price.

On your site, it's your product and your product alone. You are not losing sales to competitors when you drive traffic to your site, because even if you drive traffic to your link on an ecommerce site, customers will keep shopping on that site and may end up buying the same product from another dropshipper.

Driving traffic to your link on ecommerce is like 50/50 to you and the ecommerce company.

In addition, you can increase your price as you feel not minding competitors, but in the long run you may lose sales remembering that your customers have unrestricted access to prices on the internet.

Factors To consider when Choosing An Ecommerce Platform.

Obviously, because of the initial capital outlay, many budding dropshippers will choose an established platform, like Friend and players may also influence your decision in the field and the almighty Google.

But before jumping at one, there are many things to consider and among them are:

Cost: In dropshipping like any other business, every dollar counts and so you have to think about the platform you are going to use, whether your own or an ecommerce platform.

For ecommerce platforms, you are not in short supply and their cost range from $20 to $30 dollars a month depending on what features they parade. You could go as high as $75 if you want more features, themes and flexible customization.

For a start, start with the basic plan and scale up as you grow. When you are testing a river, you don't put your two legs at the same time.

No Of Products Allowed. Although most ecommerce platforms will allow you to list as many products as you want but some have limits.

All the same, ask them. If you intend to have many products, it won't be interesting to find out, when you are already in that you cannot list more than a couple of products.

Otunba Jide Omiyale – The Dropship Entrepreneur.

Store Design: If you own your site you can change the look anytime and this total control, to me, is the biggest advantage of owning your own site.

On the other hand, with ecommerce platforms you are limited to what they provide and usually what they provide in their basic plans may not be good enough for your business and if you want the great ones, you have to cough out more dollars.

We are back to number one above: Cost. You will really need to get informed about the total cost, so it doesn't look like shifting the goalpost after the match has started.

Features: What features are available on the platform you choose, if not on your own site?

On your own site, you can also incorporate more of this on your site, but on the big sites you are limited to what they give you, but in all honesty the big fishes among them provide all the features you may need.

You will need site security feature, inventory control, tracking, blogging, and remarketing, especially for customers who have abandoned their cart.

Until you start, unless you have done enough research, you will discover some feature you never knew before.

The Larger Picture: You have to think about the ecosystem, the larger ecommerce influence of the platform.

How easy is it to ingrate with others? Do they have their apps which expand their area of influence in the marketplace?

The Marketing Tools: Establishing the store is only one component of the problem. The last piece of the puzzle is marketing it to the intended audience.

Selecting a platform should offer you marketing and SEO capabilities to help you rank higher on search engines and attract the attention of your audience.

For instance, All in One SEO Pack, Yoast, sitemaps, Google XML and other tools could be used with WordPress WooCommerce to raise the rating of your store.

You may install SEO Optimizer, SEO Suite, SEO Booster, and other tools on Shopify to improve your search engine ranking.

Payment Options: You will want to consider the payment gateways available on the platform you want to operate because you do not want to lose sale to limited paying options. On your own site, you can incorporate as many payments option you want but on big ecommerce sites you have limited offers, but the top ones parade the popular payment options.

These are a few that you might want to think about.

Paypal.

Apple Pay.

Stripe.

Square.

Otunba Jide Omiyale – The Dropship Entrepreneur.

Google Pay.

Your card.

Support System: Now and then you need support when things wobble.

Does your ecommerce platform run a 24/7support system considering that internet commerce does not sleep?

When they are sleeping in the USA, they are busy running around awake in Europe, so its 24hours and your platform must be able to provide that.

Shipping: We cannot overemphasize the importance of prompt shipping but it does not end at just packing products in a labelled parcel and send off. It does not end until the sale is closed.

Your platform must have a flexible shipping system so as not to lose orders.

Does your platform allow air freight should I need urgent delivery for a wedding gown in just a week?

Chapter 9: The Best 5 Ecommerce Platforms To Boost Your Dropshipping.

Because dropshipping and e-commerce are similar businesses, they both employ the same kinds of e-commerce platforms. However, dropshippers should be aware of a few minor variations before launching their business, including the accessibility, costs, and, above all, the level of service provided by these companies.

Let us see how the best 5 platforms rank among themselves.

As we discussed above, there are factors you consider when you are choosing a platform for ecommerce.

It must be easy to use with minimal cost and, if possible, free with efficient 24/7 support and capability and wiliness to help you scale up.

Here are the best platforms for dropshipping as at the time of writing this report.

1. **WooCommerce:** https://woocommerce.com/

The most popular e-commerce platform in use worldwide is WooCommerce. Its market share in all e-commerce stores is close to 23 percent, and its free and simple to install plugin is largely responsible for this.

Even non-technical users can benefit greatly from WooCommerce, since it can be installed with only one click.

Otunba Jide Omiyale – The Dropship Entrepreneur.

WooCommerce is built on WordPress, the favorite platform for bloggers which allows you to have as many plug-ins as you want. It is free and you can start in minutes with a few clicks, but may be a bit difficult to navigate for a newbie on the internet.

Support is ok as they have a community, but if you run into problems, it may take some time for your tech people to come to your aid unlike when you host on paid platforms like Shopify

WooCommerce is free, and you have established dropshippers like Weber Grills, Singer, and Ripley's using it.

2. Shopify: https://www.shopify.com/

Shopify is without a doubt one of the most effective e-commerce platforms for dropshipping. It states that it hosts almost 500,000 dropshipping and e-commerce websites. They use Oberlo which they officially acquired in 2016.

Oberto is a dropshipping plugin that streamlines the process of product import and order fulfillment. Many Non-techies have found Shopify suitable for their dropshipping business.

With 19% of the market, Shopify is the second most popular platform. But it's a hosted platform, meaning you have to pay.

Shopify is a self-hosted platform which is user friendly with a lot of needed pages such as, Privacy Policy, About Us Shipping Information, Return Policy, and Shipping Calculator. It is really easy to use even for internet-greens, which may be why it is the second mostly used platform for dropshipping.

Shopify support is 24/7 via email, phone and chat.

Shopify has some marketing automation incorporated where you can send email. And SMS to engage with your customers.

This platform, unlike WooCommerce, does not come free as price ranges from $29 t0 $299 and if you want the premium, you contact them for advanced Shopify.

3 Magento. https://magento.com/

The third-most popular e-commerce platform worldwide is Magento. It may not be ideal for novices because of its complexity. Magento is developer-friendly, but necessitates at least rudimentary programming skills.

For this reason, the majority of dropshippers that use Magento as their e-commerce platform have either employed developers or have dexterity in using Magento for store development.

Magneto is free with a design that is user friendly but newbies may find it difficult to use as its design is advanced. They have support, but most are off-channels such as forums, blogs and YouTube.

For a dropshipper, you want your huddles crossed immediately with no time to be consulting videos and reading blog posts. But with about 7% of the market, some dropshippers must have seen some pluses in it.

Magneto is free and internet savvy guys may find it ideal for their dropshipping business, afterall Selco BW, JCB and Dufry host their businesses there.

4. BigCommerce: https://www.bigcommerce.com/

BigCommerce is a hosted platform like Shopify but cheaper.

Otunba Jide Omiyale – The Dropship Entrepreneur.

Many users think they may have gone after the Shopify model.

They claim to host over 150,000 websites, both large and small, and hold a sizable portion of the market for e-commerce platforms. It is renowned for having an easy-to-use interface and a speedy setup process for e-commerce. Bigcommerce does not impose transaction fees and provides an unlimited number of staff accounts.

BigCommerce is user friendly and you can get started with a trial account with themes you can easily customize.

Support is via phone, email, chat and forum just as we have in Shopify.

Like Shopify, it is not free as you have to dole out between $29 and $250 depending on the package you want.

Dropshippers using it include Nine line apparel and Marucci Sports.

5. **OpenCart:** https://www.opencart.com/

OpenCart is an easy-to-set-up, free e-commerce platform. Anyone with a basic understanding of internet knowledge may set up an OpenCart store with ease. The website also provides a number of dropshipping-related free and premium plugins and themes.

OpenCart is one of the big 5. It is user-friendly with an easy to navigate dashboard which makes it ideal for newbies. They offer support inform of tickets and forum to help users.

Prominent ecommerce enterprises such as 6 dollar shirts and British Red Cross do business with them.

Otunba Jide Omiyale – The Dropship Entrepreneur.

Bottom Line.

The question of whether to purchase a self-hosted or hosted ecommerce platform in order to launch a business is another topic of frequent discussion when ecommerce platforms are discussed.

The best we can say is: use a hosted e-commerce platform if you are not too tech-savvy and can afford it. Additionally, if you're tech savvy, choose a self-hosted e-commerce platform since it offers greater flexibility.

You see, you can employ a variety of e-commerce systems for your website. To pick the one that best suits your needs, it's crucial that you conduct some research. Make sure you have done your research before moving further.

Chapter 10: Building You Dropshipping Store And See Your Products Zoom Off The Digital Shelve.

We have dealt exhaustively with platforms to showcase your store both hosted and self-made. You have seen the pros and cons of each and the types we have.

Building an audience and selecting your product and specialty are the first steps in starting your own e-commerce business. This is an online shop where you may showcase your various products and promote sales.

Selecting the appropriate design from the outset is crucial for success, but you also need to consider how to price and organize your products to maximize sales.

There is just one main objective for e-commerce website design. Boosting sales and earnings is the goal at all times (this is arguably actually more crucial).

Of course, you also want it to look good, work well, be simple to use, and appropriately represent your brand, but all of this is really just to help you create a website that will increase sales. This implies that every component of the design of your website should be driving traffic and sales.

If it does not, it's not worth it.

Otunba Jide Omiyale – The Dropship Entrepreneur.

If you work with a reputable development business or e-commerce builder/template, you should discover that their professional experience and knowledge guide their selections, resulting in the highest potential conversion rate and earnings for you.

In this sense, investing a little extra in a reputable theme or development firm is always worthwhile.

Of course, you won't be able to compete with an entire organization made up of specialists who have the best equipment and the most expertise unless you're a professional designer yourself.

Furthermore, any amateurish website design will weaken visitor confidence in your company and decrease the likelihood that they will make a purchase.

More than any other type of design, an e-commerce store needs to appear polished and professional.

Using a WordPress theme like WooCommerce is the simplest option for most digital marketers to build their own online store.

A WordPress theme or plugin called WooCommerce may turn an entire website into an online store.

Because of this, running your store is as simple as running any other WordPress website.

In the interim, you can still have a well-designed website by purchasing a theme that you truly enjoy and that you believe will complement your brand, or by employing a group of well-versed designers to create your theme for you.

Otunba Jide Omiyale – The Dropship Entrepreneur.

As we said earlier, there are further choices. Shopify, for instance, provides you with a "hosted" e-commerce platform. This implies that, similar to a Facebook profile, for example, the website will be hosted off of your server.

After that, you direct your clients to that website so they may browse through all of your offerings.

Although this can help make things a little simpler and easier to manage, you do ultimately give up some control and flexibility over how you want to build and manage the website.

Selecting a well-known platform like one of these, Magento, or BigCommerce will ensure that you have access to a wealth of support and free themes, plugins, and other resources to aid in your sales.

Some of these capabilities, like the option to place widgets directly on your site to advertise your best products, can be really helpful. Then, go for these big players.

Chapter 11: Proven Marketing Tactics For Dropshippers.

Now you have a store with your goods displayed and waiting for sales. Sales won't happen unless you are proactive.

Many people have found out that getting the niche, the product, and setting up the store are the easiest things to do.

Getting customers to your store and consummating sales with them is the real deal. Dropshipping is so competitive that if you don't tell them where you are, nobody will ask you where you are.

Fortunately, there is a lot of information out there on how to market a store, but this soon becomes a disadvantage as you get overwhelmed and do not know which to choose.

The good thing is we have figured them out and found out those marketing tactics that work for dropshipping, which will make your store fly.

But in the long run, you will have to do a mix of free traffic, such as blogging, and paid traffic, like Instagram and Facebook.

Here we go.

Otunba Jide Omiyale – The Dropship Entrepreneur.

1. Facebook, Instagram, Google, and TikTok Ads.

Regardless of what the gurus say about marketing tactics, I have found that the quickest way to make sales on any internet model is through advertisement.

In KDP, for instance, even if you make your book as believable as the Bible, it will still be tucked in somewhere inside the pages without advertisements.

You can do keywords, SEO, blogging, and all others, which will bring in a trickle of sales, but to boost your sales as you hit the ground, you have to advertise.

So what are the channels of advertising?

Here come Facebook, Instagram, Google, and TikTok ads.

Targeted ads, unlike blogging, cost money but they bring instant results when done correctly

On Facebook, you can do $1 a day and scale up gradually.

Each different channel has its pros and cons, but it is believed that Facebook has the best ROI, even though Tik-Tok is closing up on it.

One thing about advertising, especially Facebook advertising, is that you can collect data about your customers, which will help boost your business. You know who they are, where they are, their age bracket, etc.

Nothing is cast in stone as regards which advertising medium to use or even which advertisement to use. You will need to test and find out which works best for you.

You can start with Facebook and do AB testing to find out which ad works best for you.

I have to warn that advertising is a risky business, as it's one of the surest ways to burn dollars if not done correctly. You have to monitor your spending closely, start small until you get what gives you the best ROI.

2. TikTok Marketing And IG Reels Can Make You Go Viral.

Video content works like magic. So if you are not doing TikTok and Instagram, you are leaving dollars on the table.

It is believed that a video ad converts twice as a banner ad. This is true because a viral video can give you more mileage and take you far.

While we cannot guarantee that your video will go viral, rest assured that this will add value to your marketing effort, and what's more, it is free.

You just have to learn how to do it. See YouTube below.

To make this work, post content regularly and consistently. You follow trends, and while doing this, you engage with your community.

Trends. Trends are a crucial component of any social media marketing plan, but there are a few things to consider.

First off, think about using sound effects from well-known movies, currently trending TikTok marketing, or audio from someone else's viral Instagram reels or TikTok marketing.

Otunba Jide Omiyale – The Dropship Entrepreneur.

Lastly, hashtags are included. Social media has traditionally relied heavily on hashtags as a means of organizing and locating content.

Using all the relevant trending hashtags when submitting material can increase its chances of ranking on Instagram (you can use up to 30).

Post Consistently.

You must post consistently to win your viewers' loyalty, which will build your trust and credibility.

Any internet bum knows that the algorithm favors those who are consistent.

There are ways you can schedule your posts or source them out, which costs money.

Build A Community.

Having a devoted following on social media is crucial because these users will tell their friends and family about your business, which is essentially free promotion! And word of mouth is the best form of promotion.

This is particularly crucial for dropshipping companies in areas with intense competition.

Many companies neglect to invest time in this area because interacting with your community and answering each inquiry and comment might seem laborious. However, the little work required is worthwhile.

3. Email Marketing.

Email marketing remains an indispensable tactic for any internet business model. You need customers, and one way to get them and keep them is through email.

It is free besides the cost of the software, and gurus in this business will tell you the money is in the list.

Unlike social media, where your prospective customers are cold, email marketing affords you the opportunity to warm up to them.

With email marketing, you can communicate with your audience in the comfort of their homes and offices.

The way to collect your audience's email is to either create a pop-up on your articles on your blog or create a squeeze page where you send your traffic.

While doing this, you must add a bait like a free eBook or commission for a product they buy. You must entice them with something to get them to drop their email. You set it up in such a way that they have to fill in their email to get the freebie.

Having done that, you automate the system to send those messages automatically, and you have a good deal of software out there to do this. They call it the auto-responder series.

Among them are Aweber, GetResponse, Mailchimp, and others.

There are four types of emails. The welcome email, the newsletter, the promotional email, and the festive email.

Otunba Jide Omiyale – The Dropship Entrepreneur.

Welcome Email. This is where you welcome the new prospect, and it is usually the first email he gets with his gift.

The Newsletter: An excellent way to grow your brand is through newsletters. They're a genuine and organic approach to offering value to your subscribers, such as advice and general information regarding your product, without expecting anything in return.

This strengthens your bonds with customers and fosters their trust. If you sell watches, for example, you can send them information on how to take care of their watches to keep them top-notch.

Promotional Email. It is through promotional programs that you can advertise your goods. Depending on the particular promotion, they may consist of a single email or a sequence of emails.

If you have warmed up to them enough through a newsletter, it becomes easy to sell your product to them. From the example above, you can introduce the latest fashionable watch in town.

Do not do hard-selling as many people are. You do not have to put a gun in their heads to buy from you.

Festive Email. Some dropshippers do not do this, but why not warm up to your customers during Christmas, Halloween, Black Friday, and other festivals? .

WARNING. Let me warn you here, do not spam. Do not harvest email, though you can use other people's lists with their approval. E mail marketing is another thing you have to learn, and most email companies have enough information about how to go about it when you subscribe with them.

4. Blog.

Many dropshippers sites have a blog, and you too should, and happily enough, most e-commerce sites like Shopify have a section for blogs.

If you sell on your own sites, you blog there. It sets you apart while giving you the opportunity to engage your audience.

When you blog, you can subtly sell your product,product, but you write about your niche, giving advice to your audience.

For example, if you sell a Toyota Corolla, you can blog about fuel economy and somewhere in the blog, you can say something like "Toyota for fuel economy, particularly, the Corolla", and link that to your product.s

Needless to say, you have to be current, so you keep abreast of happenings in your niche market and get such information to your audience.

The blogging software has a schedule system where you can schedule your posts ahead of time so you do not get stuck along the way.

If you use WooCommerce of WordPress, you will discover you can schedule your posts ahead and forget them, and they will appear on the blog as scheduled.

We all know that while writing blog posts, you keep in mind related keywords to make Google rank your article.

Google likes consistency. If your article comes once a week, say Mondays, keep to it without fail.

5. SEO Content Marketing For Traffic.

When doing any posting on the internet, the thing you do not forget is the keyword, which will get you ranked.

Google does the ranking as it is the number one search engine where customers go to look for items to buy or information. If Google cannot find you, then the customers will not.

The trick is to go for a little-known keyword with little or no competition to write blog posts on or post videos on, and good enough, there are keywords ranking sites, but Google keyword search and trend gives you enough information here.

In any case, most of these keyword data sites get their information from Google.

Using similar keywords across your presence on the net expands your horizon.

6. Add Reviews Of Your Product On Your Site.

It is not for nothing that sellers on the internet look for positive reviews, to the extent that some seek positive reviews fraudulently.

It has been proven that word-of-mouth recommendations are most effective. You could think that videos can be deceptive and manipulated,manipulated, but human reviews are much more respected.

Installing social proof on your site and getting positive reviews will boost your sales. These are buyers saying this product is good, and they are bound to be believed by intending customers.

You can ask for reviews through email from buyers, install a pop-up, or even give out free products for reviews, but you have to make it clear to them to give only honest reviews.

7. Concise And Catchy Descriptions:

Customers have just a few seconds to spend on your site at first, so you need to catch their attention with a catchya catchy description.

People are always in a hurry and rarely have time for long epistles, but they are attracted to witty and catchy descriptions. Customers' fleet on the internet, always have this at the back of your mind.

You learn how to write catchy descriptions through practice and by visiting the sites of successful dropshippers and seeing how they craft their descriptions. Of course, you know it is suicidal to copy them.

Hit them straight with your product's benefits, using bullet points where applicable.

If you want to show your mastery of English, wait until you write posts on your blog.

8. Easy Checkout Flow.

Come out clean with your customers from the beginning. If there are taxes to be paid, any shipping costs etc., should be communicated to them on the site well before they get to the cashing out page.

Customers do not have much time and so you should cash out as quickly as possible. The fewer steps they have to go through, the better.

Otunba Jide Omiyale – The Dropship Entrepreneur.

According to the Baynard Institute, lengthy or difficult checkout procedures cause 17% of customers to quit their carts; unsatisfactory returns cause 12%, and hidden prices account for a staggering 48% of cart abandonment.

You may not have a way around tax such as VAT, because they will be calculated based on the price at the point of pay, but let them be aware of the percentage.

Customers want to get to the cart and make one or two clicks to complete payment.

9. Influencers, You Heard About Them?

You can collaborate with influencers on social media to promote your product for a fee.

They don't produce contents, but send posts out a few times a week, not necessarily every day. They have big followers who believe them and what they say.

The influencers have engagement rates because it is the engagement that matters, not just a fleeting mention.

In this regard, an influencer with a lower number of followers, but with more active engagement, may be better than one with large followers without engagement. Find out and decide.

The way this works is that the influencer may make a video using your product and writing a review or even collaborate with another influencer.

When the posts or video is out on the platform like X (former Twitter) or Instagram, you can then hold on to this and use on your own platforms to extend the reach. More coverage for you.

Hiring an influencer costs money, which makes it necessary for you to weigh it properly.

But imagine if you can get Ronaldo to wear your wristwatch and say how cool it feels on his wrist. That goes to millions of people.

I agree, not all of us can get Ronaldo, but just get the idea.

10. Use Brand Ambassadors And Affiliates.

Brans ambassadors are like influencers, but they use your products and ask their followers to use the product. Unlike influencers, which may only review, brand ambassadors are saying they use your product and usually have a link to the product.

You either pay them or they collect commission on sales they make.

Affiliates work similarly as you have on Click bank and Amazon. They spread your links around and if they make a sale that is traced to them; they get a commission. Affiliates make up to 50% of some dropshippers for sale.

Ecommerce sites will recommend apps or software to use, but Uppromote is one of them.

11. YouTube Channel, You Need It.

One of the most cost effective marketing tactics is having a YouTube channel. You tube is the second most visited site after Google, according to Alexa ranking.

Otunba Jide Omiyale – The Dropship Entrepreneur.

Videos engage people more than anything else, especially if they are witty and interesting. It is free to make and you can get paid if YouTube advertises on your videos as a side income.

You can make interesting videos for free in Canva.

According to studies, 81% of marketers claim that using video has increased sales, and those who do not use it see a 49% slower rate of income growth.

There are factors you remember when making the video, so that internet users can get to see your video.

The following tips will help you achieve maximum user engagement: use an attention-grabbing video thumbnail to draw viewers in and add timestamps to key moments; use transcripts for blog posts or in the description; aim for maximum user engagement (the more comments and shares, the higher search engines will rank your content).

Ask them questions, give them tasks to come and comment as asking them to comment below may not be enough to engage them.

Now, you must make videos relevant to your niche. If you sell soccer training shoes, don't start making videos on woodwork.

12. Recover Abandoned Carts.

If a customer reaches the cart, it means they are almost sold, but unfortunately many customers abandon their carts. No matter how smooth the flow on your site is, you will still have abandoned carts.

To reduce this, you will have to follow our advice on easy cash out, having many pay options and making things easy at the point of pay.

Now with almost 60% of sales as almost-sold (abandoned carts) you will easily understand why it is necessary to get them back. If you can get just 50% of them to complete the journey, that will increase your sales tremendously.

And how do you do this? The best way is to automate it by sending emails to them baiting them with reduced price, free shipping and some freebies.

If your bait catches 30% of them, you would have done very well and email marketing has proven these times without number.

13. You Have To Upsell And Cross Sell.

If there is a way to increase your average basket value, then you will make more money.

It is proven that increasing the basket value of over 70% of brands by over 30% revenue.

One way to achieve this is serving personalized recommendation as part of your cash-out flow.

Another way is to recommend complimentary products, freebies and even free shipping and complimentary freebie bag for orders above a threshold.

You can say, for instance, cart up $100 you get free shipping or $10 free items.

Giving out free stuff has been a never failing marketing tactic for ages. Everybody loves free lunch.

14. Join Your Digital Communities.

Joining communities related to your niche can increase your engagement with your audience, thereby increasing your marketing space.

There you discuss the niche, ask relevant question and provide answers.

As you are an expert on your field, you should be able to offer suggestions and proffer solutions to problems.

While doing that, you subtly put a link to your blog or product.

If you hard sell, you will alienate them and this will reduce the value of advice you are giving as they see you as a guy forcing products down their throats.

If you have been on the internet for some time, you will know that Facebook, Quora, and Reddit have such groups and spaces.

Who knows, with time, you might even establish your own community.

15. Promotions, Competitions And Giveaway.

As we said earlier, people love free things, so bait your audience with freebies and gifts as promotion, competition and giveaways.

Otunba Jide Omiyale – The Dropship Entrepreneur.

You obviously have seen this offline, by conglomerates and even local companies. Buy 2 and get 3, answering some questions, often very easy to win something. We do the same in dropshipping.

These tactics increase customer loyalty, trust and opportunity for you to upsell, i.e. selling other products.

You can do this on your social media handle where existing followers share, like, and comment to expand the group.

Obviously, this will increase your community, more followers, web traffic, increase in email list and even some sales.

There are sites doing promotions and giveaways, if you do not want to use your social media handle. Some of them are ultracontests.com, truesweepstakes.com and contestgirl.com.

16. Get Good Product Photograph.

More than 90% of customers are influenced by the images of the product they are buying. That is the best appearance they can see, which is not like offline sales where the customers can hold and feel the product.

You should now understand why a sharp photograph of your product is necessary, so if the product photograph of your supplier is not satisfactory, you may need to buy a product and take some shots yourself.

For quality control, you will need to have a product as a sample anyway, so all you need is to take its photograph using a professional photographer or photograph gadgets or your phone if you have one with high resolutions.

The good thing, however, is that most suppliers have good shots of their products on their sites, which will save you money and time.

17. User Generated Content Works Like Magic.

Internet users are weary of adverts. They suspect anything that comes to them informs of ads and they immediately up their guards. This was the beginning of public relations as a profession.

The advertising industry was having problems with believability and came up with PR. The PR practitioner makes the advert not to look like one.

It is the same principle here, where the audience suspects an ad from the brand as selling but believe information from users.

In fact, they do not see it as adverts, so getting users generated content for your product will lengthen its reach.

Refer to reviews, word-of-mouth recommendation, and influencer's endorsement above.

The following tips will help you achieve maximum user engagement: use an attention-grabbing video thumbnail to draw viewers; add timestamps to key moments; use transcripts for blog posts or in the description; aim for maximum user engagement (the more comments and shares, the higher search engines will rank your content).

Otunba Jide Omiyale – The Dropship Entrepreneur.

18. Conclusion.

You will discover you have so many options here which may be overwhelming, but you can be sure each of them has been tested and proven ok.

However, you may not implement all of them otherwise you won't have time for the core business of dropshipping, after all you do not have more than 24 hours in a day.

We advise you use about 5 of the methods depending on your goal and finance and you may source some out but be careful, there are many hawks out there,

Chapter 12: Beginners Mistakes In Dropshipping.

These days with an internet connection, you can have a bite of buying and selling without having tons of money in your account.

Yes, there are still offline stores and nothing stops you from owning one, but dropshipping has made things a lot easier.

With dropshipping, you don't have to hold inventory; you do not have to have a warehouse or even a physical presence anywhere and to make it sweet, you can start with very little capital, sometimes as low as $200.

But with all these advantages of dropshipping, many practitioners of the model still make mistakes, some of which may grievously harm their business.

We have below some mistakes to avoid whether you are green in the business or have been there for years.

By reading these mistakes, you avoid the pits many people have fallen into along the way.

1. Too High Expectations:

Many people enter the droshipping business expecting to make tons of money overnight.

Usually, they get this idea having watched some videos on You Tube or reading a course on 'how to make millions from

Otunba Jide Omiyale – The Dropship Entrepreneur.

drpshipping' often written by those who do not know anything about ecommerce.

Pronto, they have set up a site, have a product they fancy and expect dollars to start rolling in.

One, two months along the line, they have made a couple of sales and they quit. Dropshipping is a scam, they say.

Things aren't like that. In fact, dropshipping is a business model that has changed lives of many when done properly.

Like all other internet models, you have to do it right, work hard, work consistently and grow gradually. This model does not make you Elon Musk overnight, but if you are ready to put in the sweat, it will reward you financially.

So the first mistake is to think you become a millionaire tomorrow, but the moment you are realistic, you are good to go.

2. Too Much Research.

Research you must do. In fact, it is suicidal to jump into this business without research. However, overdoing it is a mistake made by many.

You can never research to the extent of eliminating mistakes, as mistakes are part of the learning process. Research a bit and start and earn along the way.

If the sculptor spends too much time on the nose of his object, the nose will soon be obliterated.

Strive to strike a balance when doing your research. Gain a solid understanding of dropshipping fundamentals from the available materials in and out of this book, but keep in mind that you'll learn a lot via experience and that you'll never know everything.

True, if you research for ages, you will not make mistakes because you won't start, but then you will not make any money.

3. Inadequate Product Research.

Not doing enough research is as bad as wasting too much time on research.

But how would one just jump at dropshipping without research you ask, but some people do it?

Just pick a product they fancy, set up a store and expecting sales to roll in not bothered about whether that product will sell or not.

You have to do research and find out whether the product is selling, does it have enough profit margin, and what is the competition like?

If there is too much competition, the big players can stiff you, but if the competition is high and the market values are large enough, you can still go in and have a bite.

The surest thing is to have a moving product with little competition, that way you shorten your success graph.

Otunba Jide Omiyale – The Dropship Entrepreneur.

4. Covering Too Much Ground.

Going into every niche is a sure recipe for failure. You need to find your niche and concentrate on your niche.

A niche is a specialized market in which you will operate. You may think that being the dropshipping equivalent of Amazon is the way to go because more variety could lead to more customers, but I tell you, it does not happen like that.

You are not Amazon, so you cannot sell everything, but many dropshippers make this mistake thinking the more they cover the merrier.

If you are in training shoes niche, you could niche down to boy's training shoes to be specific.

Choose your specialty, refer to how to select a niche and product above.

5. Choosing The Wrong Niche.

Choosing the appropriate niche is one of the most important dropshipping considerations.

Instead of considering market demand while selecting a niche, novices frequently make the error of picking a niche anyhow. It's critical to carry out in-depth research to find lucrative niches with enough demand.

You want to get the niche right bearing in mind profitability, competition, high sales volume, etc.

You must get your niche and product right.

Otunba Jide Omiyale – The Dropship Entrepreneur.

6. Supplier's Reliability.

Stock outs, low product quality, and delayed delivery are just a few of the problems that can arise from depending on untrustworthy suppliers.

To make sure a supplier is trustworthy and able to fulfill demand, beginners should conduct a complete background check on them.

Choose supplier rightly.

7. Putting Too Much Trust On A Supplier.

This business, like others, requires you to have some degree of trust in your partners. You depend on them to do many important things for you, like packing, shipping and timely delivery.

Earlier we discussed some red flags you check for in suppliers

Again, relying on a supplier may raise some issues, so it may be wise to have substitutes.

In the long run, it may be a good business practice to enter into an agreement with your suppliers with well spelt out terms and conditions.

8. Price Undercutting.

Beginners think that low price means more sales, yes it could mean more sales, but it is coming back to bite your bum.

A deal that seems too good to be true usually is, and cheap pricing will convince customers they're buying an inferior product (even if your product is the same as the competition).

As a dropshipper, charging much less than the competition tends to turn off potential clients.

If you cut price, the customers may think your product is inferior to others, because if not, why so low? And besides, low price will cut into your profit.

In dropshipping, more sales from price cut may not mean more profit. But new dropshippers make this mistake. You need to avoid it.

9. Neglecting Customer Reviews And Feedback:

Eliminating the need for product manufacturing, warehouse storage, and customer shipment is one of dropshipping many advantages.

You act as a go-between for the provider and the client.

Dropshippers frequently believe they may disregard client comments and evaluations as a result.

After all, the carrier has responsibility for any lost or damaged goods, not you?

Not precisely. Even if the supplier is ultimately to blame for delivery issues, customers identify with you as the firm that deals with the public.

Because of this, you are far more affected by their errors than you may think. Note the criticism. Get in touch with the supplier if a customer has an issue and assist to it.

10. No Optimized Website:

A badly designed website with a challenging user's experience or sluggish loading times may turn potential buyers off.

To improve the users' experience, new entrants should give top priority to developing a website that is visually appealing, mobile-responsive, and easy to navigate.

You cannot afford to make a scrappy website and expect sales. The site is your shop and you have to make it as beautiful as possible.

It must be optimized to make visitors experience flawless.

Easy navigation and with few pop-ups, probably as visitors want to exit the site.

We are saying this because many green dropshopper are wont to rush to put something up usually going to freelance sites like Fiver or Upwork to get their sites done. Usually they will go for cheap ones and is then you know you get what you pay.

A man charging $10 to make a site will most likely give you a scrappy site.

You are not likely to have this problem if you use ecommerce sites like Shopify. We discussed this earlier on.

11. No Marketing Plan.

Without a thorough marketing plan, simply displaying things on a website can result in little traffic and revenues. In order to draw clients and establish a distinctive brand, beginners need to put time and effort into branding and marketing.

You need to spend resources on your marketing plan and know how to navigate the forest of tactics from the beginning. Optimizing SEO is good but it cannot do the magic, you need a concerted marketing plan.

You are lucky. You can refer to marketing tactics for Dropshippers in this book.

12. Using Unethical SEO Practices (Black Hat).

You may be tempted to use unethical SEO to rank your site and there a lot of them out there promising you heaven and earth with magical SEO tricks otherwise referred to as black hat SEO.

While they may help you initially, they will come back to hurt you. Google cannot be deceived for long.

Eventually, it will catch you and punish you. I have tried to cut corners before and I got hurt.

Play by the rules.

It's always better to play by the rules in this business.

13. Using Influencers:

Another common mistake new entrants into dropshpping make is to think that they can overrun competitors by using influencers on the social media early.

While using influencers on social media like Instagram, TikTok and X may be a viable option as marketing tactic for established concerns, it may be counterproductive for a new dropshipper.

Social media influencers don't come cheap as those with many followers may charge exorbitantly, which may burn holes in the pocket of a new dropshipper.

Caution is the word here.

14. No Established System For Returns.

No matter how great your product is and no matter how big you are, you will have returns. Even AliExpress and Amazon do have returns to deal with.

As a dropshipper, you may think that dealing with returns is the problem of your supplier, yes you may be right, but it's your reputation at stake here. It's you the customer is dealing with and it's you he knows.

Therefore, you would want to follow up his returns and make sure your supplier handles it speedily to your customer's satisfaction.

Customers well treated this way are likely going to come back again, knowing very well that if he returns a product, it will be changed, or he gets a refunded.

15. Inadequate Financial Planning and Monitoring:

Inadequate monitoring of costs, earnings, and cash flow might result in financial troubles. To guarantee that the business maintains a sound financial position, new dropshippers should put in place reliable financial monitoring methods and carefully prepare their budget.

16. Disregarding Tax and Legal Responsibilities

Newcomers frequently fail to consider the tax and legal ramifications of operating a dropshipping company. To prevent future problems, it is essential to comprehend the legal requirements, such as business licenses, and the tax duties related to the firm.

17. Not Taking Holidays Into Consideration.

There are holidays like Black Friday, Christmas, New Year in the USA and other holidays in other countries.

Make a plan, consult the calendar, and ensure that you are promoting your products around the holidays when applicable. You can increase sales even on smaller holidays or on sporadic novelty days.

You must plan for these holidays and take advantage of them and may even give them discounts.

Many beginners do not do this and thereby leave a lot of cash on the table.

18. Dropping Off Early.

This dropshipping business is a bus on a long journey and only the strong will get to the end. New entrants often find out that the dollar rains don't happen as the YouTube gurus tell them and they chicken out early.

Dropshipping model like other business models require hard work, commitment, dedication. You learn new tricks, build your infrastructure and try new ideas.

You do not just set the site up with few products and expect dollars to fill your account.

No, it doesn't work like that. You earn what you work for.

Chapter 13: Prohibited and Restricted Items.

Usually, the sites recommended will not promote prohibited items on their sites, but you can never tell. Some may slip though the vetting system, so it's better for you to know what you can and cannot bring in to your country.

You will need to find out those things you cannot import into a country you want to do business in, whether in your own or another.

The seller has not much at stake again. It's you bringing in the items and so it's your responsibility to ensure you are not breaking any law.

For this guide, we will list those items prohibited in the United States of America and Nigeria.

Note that there is a difference between prohibited and restricted.

Prohibited means you cannot bring them in, while restriction means you may bring them in under certain conditions. You will need to find out.

Otunba Jide Omiyale – The Dropship Entrepreneur.

When importing from China, it is very important to understand the system and procedure to ensure you get the right products at a very good bargain.

This is more important if you are doing this as business because at ultimately the profit will sustain the business.

As a personal buyer, you also need to make the right decisions to keep up the excitement and the value derived from your money and effort.

You may need to take it a notch up by opening an account purposely for this. And along this line, you may want to open a virtual business account to separate the transactions from others.

The USA.

On U.S. Custom and boarder protection site, these are the prohibited and restricted items.
https://www.cbp.gov/travel/us-citizens/know-before-you-go/prohibited-and-restricted-items#:~:text=Examples%20of%20prohibited%20items%20are,to%20enter%20the%20United%20States.

From the page.
'Examples of prohibited items are dangerous toys, cars that don't protect their occupants in a crash, bush meat, or illegal substances like absinthe and Rohypnol. Restricted means that special licenses or permits are required from a federal agency before the item is allowed to enter the United States. Examples of restricted items include firearms, certain fruits and vegetables, animal products, animal byproducts, and some animals'

Otunba Jide Omiyale – The Dropship Entrepreneur.

1. Absinthe (alcohol)
2. Alcoholic beverages.
3. Automobiles.
4. Biological material.
5. Ceramic tableware.
6. Cultural artifacts and cultural property.
7. Defense articles or items with military and proliferation applications.
8. Dog and cat fur.
9. Drug paraphernalia.
10. Firearm.
11. Fish and wildlife.
12. Food products (raw and prepared)
13. Fruits and vegetable.
14. Game and hunting trophies
15. Gold.
16. Haitian animal hide drums.
17. Medications.
18. Merchandise from embargoed countries.
19. Pets.
20. Photographic films.
21. Plants and seeds.
22. Soil.
23. Trademark and copyrighted articles.

Nigeria.

Absolutely Prohibited Goods

(These Are Completely No Go Areas)

1. Air Pistols
2. Airmail Photographic Printing Paper.
3. All counterfeit/pirated materials or articles including Base or Counterfeit Coin of any Country.
4. Beads composed of inflammable celluloid or other similar substances.
5. Blank invoices.
6. Coupons for Foreign Football pools or other betting arrangements.

7. Cowries.
8. Exhausted tea or tea mixed with other substances
9. Implements appertaining to the reloading of cartridges.
10. Indecent or obscene prints, painting, books, cards, engraving or any indecent or obscene articles.
11. Manilas.
12. Matches made with white phosphorous.

13. Materials of any description with a design which, considering the purpose for which any such material is intended to be used, is likely in - the opinion of the president to create a breach of the peace or to offend the religious views of any class of persons in Nigeria.

14. Meat, Vegetables or other provisions declared by a health officer to be unfit for human consumption.

15. Piece goods and all other textiles including wearing apparel, hardware of all kinds' crockery and china or earthenware goods bearing inscriptions (whether in Roman or Arabic characters) from the Koran or from Courtesy Nigerian Customs Services the traditions and commentaries on the Koran.

16. Pistols disguised in any form.

17. Second-hand clothing.

18. Silver or metal alloy coins not being legal tender in Nigeria.

19. Nuclear Industrial waste and other Toxic waste

20. Spirits: -

13. Weapons of any description which in the opinion of the Comptroller-General are designed for the discharge of any noxious liquid, gas or other similar substance and any ammunition containing or in the opinion of the Comptroller-General or adapted to contain any noxious liquid, gas or other similar substances

Otunba Jide Omiyale – The Dropship Entrepreneur.

Courtesy Nigerian Customs Service.

Importation Prohibition List
(No Go Areas With Exceptions)

1. Live or Dead Birds including Frozen Poultry
2. Pork, Beef
3. Birds Eggs
4. Refined Vegetable Oils and Fats
5. Cocoa Butter, Powder and Cakes
6. Spaghetti/Noodles
7. Fruit Juice in Retail Packs
8. Waters, including Mineral Waters and Aerated Waters containing added Sugar or Sweetening Matter or Flavored, ice snow
9. Bagged Cement
10. Medicaments falling under Headings 3003 and 3004.
11. Waste Pharmaceuticals
14. Sanitary Wares of Plastics.
15. Rethreaded and used Pneumatic tires but excluding used trucks tyres for rethreading of sized 11.00 x 20 and above 4012.2010.00.
16. Corrugated Paper and Paper Boards
17. Telephone Re-charge Cards and Vouchers
18. Textile Fabrics of all types and articles thereof and Yarn
19. All types of Foot Wears and Bags including Suitcases of leather and plastics
20. Hollow Glass Bottles of a capacity exceeding 150mls (0.15 litres) of a kind used for packaging of beverages by breweries and other beverage and drink companies
21. Used Compressors – H.S. Code 8414.3000, Used Air Conditioners
23. Ball Point Pens

Courtesy Nigerian Customs Services.

CREDIT. From our book. *How To Import From China.*

Chapter 14: How To Register Your Business.

Actually, many people do dropshipping business under their named but ultimately as your business grows you will consider registering a company.

The process differs from country to country. You will need to find out how to register a business in your country.

In the USA, it depends on your state. Please find out.

In Nigeria, you register with the Corporate Affairs Commission of Nigeria https://pre.cac.gov.ng/home

Choosing Your Business Name:

Picking a business can be daunting, as you need to get a name that synchronizes with the products you want to sell.

Besides, you have to establish that such a name is not being used by another person, whether in the registrar of companies or the social media.

It must be short and easy to remember.

Company Structure.

One thing you have to decide is the structure of your company. Is it a sole proprietorship, a limited liability company, or a partnership? Most people start as sole proprietorship.

Otunba Jide Omiyale – The Dropship Entrepreneur.

Registering Your Business Name.

Once you are through with a business name, you go ahead to register it with your country's registrar of companies. Of course, you will need to find out if another person has not taken such a name.

Most companies have their register where you can search and make sure the name is free to use.

You will also need to make sure that it has not yet been registered with any of the registrars on the net as you may need to register its .com or whatever your branded URL is. You can easily verify this on their sites.

Employer Identification Number (EIN):

As a company, you will need the employer identification number. This protects your social security number in the USA and separates the company from you as a legal person. Your company can then hire people and build its own credit.

In the USA, you can get this done on their IRS site.

It is important to note that each locality may require different requirements. It's your responsibility to find out what operates where you are running your business pertaining to taxes such as VAT and slates tax.

If you are operating as an individual, you need the individual Tin (ITIN).

1. Tin No. You can hardly do business on the net, especially when the USA is concerned without the TIN number. For

sure, you cannot open a bank account without a TIN number.

Requirements may differ from the country, but they have similar requirements. You will need to find out the requirements for your country. In the USA, they are usually 9 digits while it's 8 in Nigeria.

In the USA, to obtain an ITIN, you must complete IRS Form W-7, IRS Application for Individual Taxpayer Identification Number. The Form W-7 requires documentation substantiating foreign/alien status and true identity for each individual.

This is the site for USA
https://www.irs.gov/individuals/international-taxpayers/taxpayer-identification-numbers-tin#:~:text=To%20obtain%20an%20ITIN%2C%20you,true%20identity%20for%20each%20individual.

Tax site in Nigeria is here: https://tinverification.jtb.gov.ng/

To get your TIN (Taxpayer Identification Number), you typically need to follow these steps:

Visit the nearest BIR office nearest to you, the list of which you get on their site. In the USA, you can do it by mail or through an IRS-authorized Acceptance Agent or Certified Acceptance Agent.

2. In the BIR office, ask for the Tin form and complete it.

3. Obviously you will need to submit some documents and some form of identification such as driving license, passport or social security number.

4. After submission, wait for them to process.

Otunba Jide Omiyale – The Dropship Entrepreneur.

5. Once you are through, you get your TIN number, whether through mail or in person.

Remember, it's important to keep your TIN in a safe place like on your computer, as you'll need it now and then when doing business on the internet and even off-line activities such as opening a bank account.

Chapter 15: Dropshipping With Amazon

Amazon dropshipping is similar to normal dropshiping, the only difference being that you do it with Amazon. You as a seller, list your products with Amazon. When you make a sale, you purchase the product from a supplier who supplies to your customer directly.

You will notice that here too, you do not hold inventory. As we proceed, you will see the minor differences between the normal dropshiping and Amazon dropshipping.

We have singled out amazon because of the size, popularity, coverage and turn over.

Amazon.com had roughly 2.27billion combined web visits in December 2023 and a net income of about nine billion US dollars.

Conditions To Fulfill To Allow You Dropship On Amazon.

You must be the sole and only seller of the product.

On the packaging, on the invoice and other documents pertaining to that product must be in your name.

There must be no information pertaining to the third party (supplier) on the product to prevent confusion.

Of course you must abide strictly with Amazon seller agreement and policy on dropshipping.

Otunba Jide Omiyale – The Dropship Entrepreneur.

You will be in charge of handling returns.

Advantages Of Amazon Dropshipping.

- Amazon has vetted dropshipping suppliers who are reputable and so new sellers have not much problem in choosing suppliers.
- Amazon gives you incredible discoverability with exhaustive product categories with many niches, meaning you can get to large targeted audience.
- Amazon SEO is top-notch therefore you are covered here. Of course you will still need to do some marketing.

Disadvantages of Amazon Dropshipping.

- You do not have control over your data. Amazon uses your sales data to her advantage.
- You have few connections with your customers. Amazon is bothered more about sales that your relationship building. This is a big disadvantage.
- Customization is under amazon control. You cannot really stand on your own with this model.

Steps To Starting Dropshipping In Amazon.

- The first thing is to set up an Amazon Selling Account. Visit [Seller Central account](). Amazon has all the tools you need.
- Choose a product to sell and here you may need amazon approval for some products.
- Source for a supplier. In this book, we have discussed what to look for in a supplier and the red flags to look for. Better to choose a supplier who has worked with amazon sellers before.
- **List your product on amazon.**

Otunba Jide Omiyale – The Dropship Entrepreneur.

- ✓ Sell and grow your store. There are resources for you by Amazon to sell and grow your business.
- ✓ Promote your store. We discussed marketing extensively to those, you may add amazon standard product advertising.

Amazon Dropshipping And Amazon FBA.

Both are fulfillment models where you sell products without holding inventory.

In FBA (Fulfillment By Amazon), amazon holds the inventory, pack and ship the products while in dropshipping neither you nor amazon holds inventory.

Conclusion

Amazon dropshipping with FBA is a business model of its own. It needs studying. You must be ready to be committed and resilient and you may need some initial capital outlay.

Chapter 16: Important KPIs For Tracking Dropshipping Profitability

Being precise is not just a catchphrase in dropshipping; it's the roadmap to success. The real deal comes from the reliable and actionable data you collect from the key performance indicators (KPI)

If you are ready to learn the measurements that will either make or break your dropshipping business, we are ready to take you down the road, so let us go.

What are Key Performance Indicators (KPI)?

They are indicators or figures you use to measure how well your dropshipping business is doing. When used properly, they let you know whether you are achieving the goals set for your business.

This is understandable because, in the physical retail business, they keep books from where they monitor their business. They have metrics like return on investment. (ROI), cost of sales (COS), sales revenues and others. Without them, you cannot know where adjustments need to be made.

For instance, if it is your desire to increase monthly sales revenue, you will need to look at monthly revenue KPI. This figure will show you how many sales you have made in that month and by what percentage you will have to increase them.

What Role Does KPI Play In Your Dropshipping Success?

KPIs are vital in this business. They are like the vitals the doctors check when you visit them.

KPIs provide an objective view of the health of your dropshipping business. For example, if you need to know the cost per lead (CPL), you will want to know how much it costs you to get a lead in the email campaign. If it's too high, you develop steps to cut down on the cost of email campaign without losing its effectiveness.

Keeping an eye on your KPIs leads to increased profit because you can see where the house is leaking and block the leakages. For example, by analyzing your return rate, you will see why products are being returned, and you can fix the issues. If your cart abandonment is on the rise, you will see why and fix issues, perhaps your product quality is decreasing.

KPI monitoring ensures your decisions are data driven and enables you to respond quickly to customer behavior and changes in the market and be more competitive.

So what are the KPIs to keep? There are many, but we will discuss those that have a very direct impact on the dropshipping business.

Sales Revenue.

In accounting, when drawing the profit-and-loss account, the first entry is the total sales. In KPI, the first indicator to measure has got to be the total revenue accruing to the business over a period.

Otunba Jide Omiyale – The Dropship Entrepreneur.

It is very fundamental to keep records of sales made over a period of time. At first, you may think you can do it on your own, but with time, you will need software to track it.

Getting this data is not as important as analyzing it. Data is useless if you have not put it to use.

Measuring sales revenue helps you set a benchmark. If, for example, last year you made a sale of $20000, you may want to increase it by 20% to $25000.

Average Order Value.

This is the average revenue you generate from one order. For example, if you generate $1000 from 100 orders, your average order value is $10. You get this by dividing $1000 by 100. If you up this, even marginally, you increase your profit and what we call customer lifetime values.

If for example, you get 800 visits per month with a 5% conversion rate; you get 40 sales. Now, with an average order value of $200, you have a revenue of $8000. If you can increase this to just $230 AOV, your revenue goes to $9200, bringing in an extra $1200 without spending extra on attracting more customers.

Calculating Customer Lifetime Value (CLV Or LTV)

This measures the amount of money you expect a customer to spend with you throughout their relationship with you.

In a healthy situation, this should be at least 3x of the cost of customer acquisition. (CAC)

Otunba Jide Omiyale – The Dropship Entrepreneur.

If you track this metric monthly or annually, as many do, you get a clear idea of your LTV trend, and improving on this trend enhances faster repurchase rates by customers.

Monitoring Conversion Rate.

You should understand that several factors, such as website design, ease of navigation, clarity of messages, and customer reviews on the site to build prospecting customers' confidence, will influence the conversion rate.

Tools like Google analytics will help you know at what stage your visitors become hesitant and you can make adjustments.

You must refine this regularly to fine-tune your site to enhance the customer experience and thereby increase sales.

Customer Acquisition Cost (CAC)

CAC refers to the cost of acquiring a customer. This cost includes the cost of advertising, salespeople's salaries, cost of software for marketing, etc.

One-time CAC is the cost spent per customer to make the first purchase, while long-term CAC is the total cost for the time the customer is with your business, which may decrease with time. You can see the importance of the LTV metric discussed above. The longer the LTV, the greater the likelihood of the CAC coming down.

If you spend $100 to acquire a customer, it may decrease with longer LTV.

By monitoring this over time, you will know if your spending is bringing in commensurate customers, and if not, you will adjust accordingly.

Otunba Jide Omiyale – The Dropship Entrepreneur.

Cost Per Lead.

The total cost to get a prospective customer by providing their email or phone number is called the cost per lead. This is usually obtained when you entice a customer with a gift for their contact information. (See email marketing)

This differs from CAC, which is the cost of getting the order.

Monitoring your CPL will let you know the efficiency and cost effectiveness of your campaigns. It lets you know effect of increased advertising and effect of seasons and holidays which allows you plan for the future.

You can do A/B campaigns based on channels, advertisement creative.

Capturing this information of your customer has a longtime positive effect on your business. Gurus say the money is in the list.

Cart Abandonment Rate.

Cart abandonment is an enormous challenge in e-commerce, even for giant players like Amazon and AliExpress.

This matrix measures the percentage of shoppers who drop off at the check-off stage. By analyzing this indicator, you will know at what stage most of them abandon cart and the reasons for this.

For example, if a significant number of customers abandon because of shipping costs, you may need to reevaluate this. You may want to offer a discounted rate or do free shipping for a certain amount of order.

Temu does this trick to their advantage. They tell you to get free shipping for orders above a certain amount.

As a solution, you could send a discounted code, as they are about to abandon. There are many ways to kill a rat.

Gross Profit Margin Indicator.

The whole thing starts here. If your gross profit is low, it will surely affect your net profit, so you have to watch this.

Gross profit, therefore, is a profitability indicator.

You get your gross profit by subtracting the cost of goods from the selling price. If you sell a product for $100 and you get it for $60, your gross margin is $40, which is 40%. All other expenses, such as advertising and promotion, will reduce this amount until you have the net profit left.

How do you use this indicator? You benchmark it against others. If your margin is significantly lower than the industry margin, you have to do something. You may need to negotiate a lower price with your supplier, watch the shipping cost, or do a bundle deal that encourages customers to buy more at a time.

Conclusion.

If you keep an eye on these KPIs, you may more precisely forecast client behavior and purchasing patterns, which will allow you to alter your strategies to make your business more profitable and competitive.

Chapter 17: A Dropshipping Case Study.

We have done a lot of theory. It is time to put what we have learned into practice.

Let us start a dropshipping process from the beginning and have a feel of it.

Getting A Niche And Product.

The first thing is to get a niche and the product to sell.

To remind you, you don't just sell watches, but what kind of watch are you selling? You have to niche down. You may want to refer to "how to choose a dropshipping niche and product" discussed earlier.

Are you selling women's watches or boy's watches or a particular brand? Will you be going for Led watches and if you are going for led watches, is it with steel strap? Leather strap or rubber strap. You have to niche down and be specific.

Obviously, you may have many markets you are interested in, but as you know you cannot do all and before that, you must have some no-go areas in this business.

Theoretically, you can dropship any product, but some endear themselves to this business more than others for some obvious reasons.

I would not like to dropship the following products.

Otunba Jide Omiyale – The Dropship Entrepreneur.

1. Food, for instance, may be out of the way as you may not guarantee the quality.

2. Electronics may get spoilt during shipment, and this may result in refunds from unsatisfied customers. I once imported a foot massager which did not work when received. There was no way to test when buying, as this could have been a manufacturing error.

3. Heavy items for obvious reasons of shipping cost.

I prefer low-priced items with free shipping. Low-priced item so I would not lose much money in case of refund. And free shipping for obvious reasons.

Having spent time on my search, I have decided on Water Shoes.

You can see that there are different shoes but we have niched down to water shoes.

My product is light, low-priced and not likely to get damaged during shipment and would endear to free shipping. And it is unisex even though we can niche down to men, kids and women.

We got this product having researched the best sellers on Amazon, Temu, AliExpress and Etsy. Good enough, they all have water shoes in their best sellers.

Let us see the results they returned.

1. Amazon.
https://www.amazon.com/gp/bestsellers

Otunba Jide Omiyale – The Dropship Entrepreneur.

On this bestsellers page on Amazon, all the products have low BSR, meaning the product is moving very fast. Look at these two, 41 and 8 and not expensive meeting our requirements.

By the way, if you are not used to Amazon parameters, the lower the BSR of a product, the more the sales of that product. In our example here, the product with BSR of 8 sells more than that of 41, but both are fast selling products.

Again, see the number of reviews and the ratings. These tell us the product is not only satisfactory but also in demand.

Considering the ranking of Amazon, I am not surprised these products did well in other validations.

2. Lightinthehouse.
http://www.lightinthebox.com/c/best-sellers-511_72965

Water shoes was also returned among the best sellers of lightinthehouse.com.

Otunba Jide Omiyale – The Dropship Entrepreneur.

3.Temu.   https://www.temu.com/channel/best-sellers.html?

4.AliExpress
https://www.AliExpress.com/w/wholesale-top-ranking-products.html?spm=a2g0o.home.history.2.650c76dbF2LjQu

This product is top selling.

Otunba Jide Omiyale – The Dropship Entrepreneur.

See AliExpress return. Over 1000 sold with 4.7 score with a price of about $9. The price of NGN10,876 is in naira which gives you about $9.

5. Etsy

https://www.etsy.com/market/best_selling_items

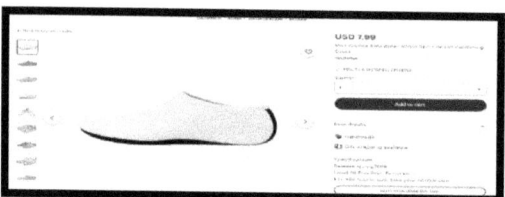

Validation.

We have chosen our product which is a bestselling product from our research. Now we have to validate it to ensure that it will sell.

We do the validation with Google using Google Trend and social media.

Otunba Jide Omiyale – The Dropship Entrepreneur.

Google Trends   https://trends.google.com/trends/

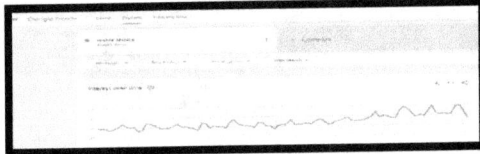

This trend had neen on the increase in the last 90 days. I am not surprised becasu of the amazon BSR

Social Media Validation

#1. Instagram
Typing water shoes in instagram returned encouraging results with many hashtags for the keyword.
#watershoes for kids
#watershoes are cool
#watershoesswag
#watershoesformen
#watershoesforwmen

#2: Facebook
Inserting the following keyword in Facebook search returned overwhelming posts. This means this keyword is popular and people are looking for water shoes.
"water shoes "just pay shipping"
"water shoes "order now""

Otunba Jide Omiyale – The Dropship Entrepreneur.

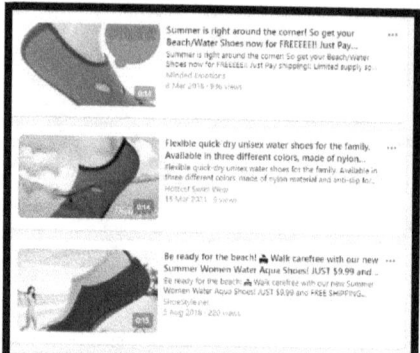

#3.Twitter (X)

In order to get a real view of the engagements on twitter, we used a site called Keyhole.co.. it gave us the result below.

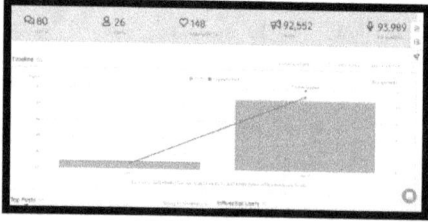

Over a period of twenty four hours, 26 users posted 80 tweets with the term "water shoes". This is encouraging.

Otunba Jide Omiyale – The Dropship Entrepreneur.

Twitter is alo encouraging. There were many tweets meaning we can get people to tweet and retweet for us.

Conclusion.

We have validated our product on Instagram, Twitter and Facebook which means we can proceed, because they are the best media for our business. We could go for Reddit but you will find out that these three are enough besides just making a presence on Reddit or Pinterest

Coming Up With a Name and a Logo.

Some people may find it difficult to get a name and logo for their dropshipping business but the internet can help.

Remember you have to get a name that is short, relevant and easy to remember.

To help us let us go to the site
https://www.oberlo.com/tools/business-name-generator.

From there we got this.

Otunba Jide Omiyale – The Dropship Entrepreneur.

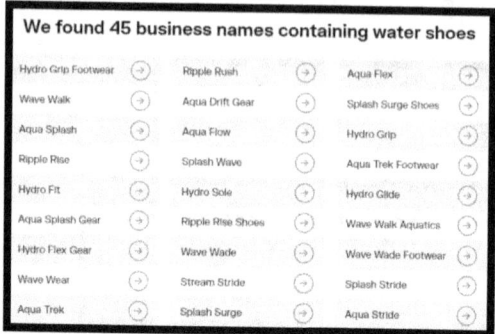

We pick Aqua Flex. Aqua is the French word for water which makes it interesting.

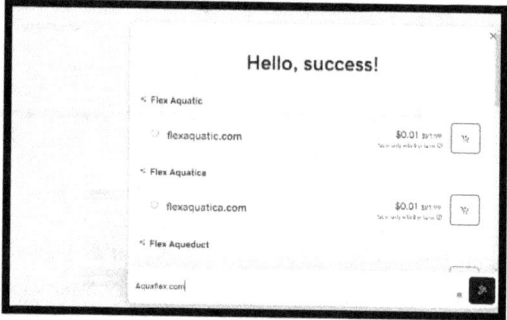

We now go to Godaddy to see if the .com domain is available and we are lucky it is available.   Aquaflex.com.

We can now proceed with our logo. Here we go to wix logo maker for assistance. https://manage.wix.com/logo/maker

You can also use canva.

Otunba Jide Omiyale – The Dropship Entrepreneur.

Below is the logo we got from wix logo maker, a free software. It's not the best, but it will serve,

If you can afford it, you may ask professionals to get it done for you for a fee on Fiver or Up work.

Building The Store.

We have our product which we have validated with Google trend and 3 major social media platforms. We have given our store a name with a .com extension and a logo.

The next thing is to build our store, but from here we will only explain as it will involve money and would not want to spend money on a store we don't want to run.

If you refer "to how to start a dropshiping store", you will discover you have two choices.

You either pick an established e-commerce company or you have your own site.

Clever dropshippers will go for an established ecommerce company, but this does not mean you will not have a blog with your registered domain.

WooCommerce is the biggest e-commerce company followed by Shopify. With WooCommerce you will have to build the store yourself in Wordpress and this may be too tasking for a man just starting internet business, but in Shopify you have a friend with built in sites with no tech knowledge.

So, we will advise you to go with Shopify.

They have many templates and themes to choose from and you just follow the prompts and you have a site for your dropshipping business.

And if you need to add images, you can easily go to Pixabay, Freepik and Burst for free images and if you have the money, you can get paid images from Stock Photos.

When setting up your stores, do not forget to put in these core pages.

These are terms of service (TOS), contact us, this is a must, refund and privacy policy.

Since we are offering free shipping, we must set the setting to free shipping.

You have to include Facebook pixel and Google analytics integrations to monitor your traffic

You will also have to install some apps too and as you are using Shopify, Oberlo is a must. You may also need to install Spocket.

From these you will be importing goods to your store. Spocket is integrated with AliExpress one of the biggest ecommerce stores.

There are others you can integrate as well, such as Dsers-Aliepress Dropshipping, Sup Dropshipping, Dropshipman and a host of others.

Otunba Jide Omiyale – The Dropship Entrepreneur.

You may also source your suppliers, but these companies parade suppliers they have vetted and in who they have utmost trust when it comes to integrity, reliability and products quality.

So that you may know, you can create marketing automation in Shopify. With this you can send your customers multichannel messages through SMS, email and push notifications to build relationship with them. Doing this will boost engagements with your customers, which will result in more sales.

Payment Gateway.
Of course, you have to install the payment gateway.
PayPal Express and Stripe your best bet.

Description.

The description of your product is very important. You can copy from your supplier and rewrite. Don't just copy and paste because the internet will find out. There are many softwares out there for rewriting and make it original to you.

Since you know your keywords (From Google and Amazon) which you would have gotten from your research, you put them in their search bars and bring the goods to your store.

About keywords, if you enter "water shoes" into Amazon search bar you have over 40 keywords. See some below.

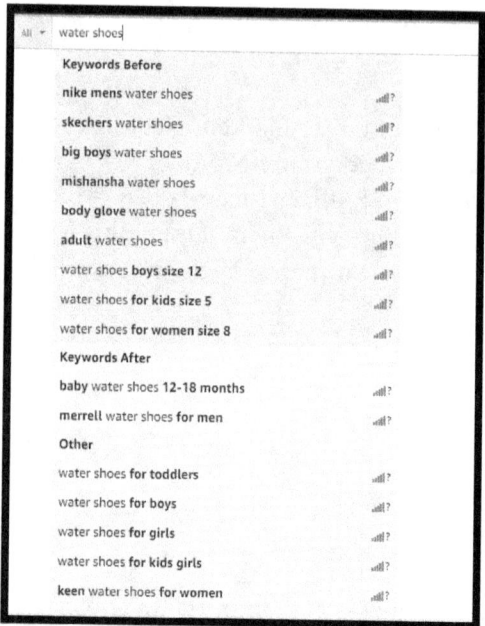

Marketing.

We dealt with this extensively in the body of this book, but I need to chip in some nuggets.

No matter how good your product is, nobody will ask you about it until you tell them about it. Organic traffic is good, especially if you have a blog which we recommend, but it's not enough.

You will need other media like Facebook and especially, Instagram.

Otunba Jide Omiyale – The Dropship Entrepreneur.

Email

You will be doing your business a lot of good to incorporate email marketing into your promotion.

All internet gurus agree on something- the money is in the list. You must build a list and the only way to do this is through email marketing.

You will need to subscribe with the email companies like GetResponse, MailChimp, Aweber, and many others out there, with each of them offering enough tutorial to get you going.

They will show you how to set up your squeeze and landing pages to capture the data of your customers.

The joy in this is that you may even sell to them items different from the one in your site when you have sufficiently wormed up to them.

Facebook.

For e-commerce business owners, Facebook advertising is typically the best marketing channel because it produces a high return on investment (ROI).

This is incredibly valuable for dropshippers, as you may guess.

All we need to do is to install the Facebook pixel and a Facebook page and start a few minor campaigns.

The page does not have to be elaborate, just something solid and reputable to your customers.

Blogging.

If you are taking this as a serious business, you will need a blog where you write articles on your niche and direct readers there.

One advantage of this is that if you post regularly, you can install Google ad to earn you more money.

You can also put your landing and squeeze pages, and it's not expensive to set this up.

You use your registered domain to set it with a free word press theme and start posting. If you find this a hard task, you can source this out for a couple of dollars on Fiver or Upwork.

Pricing.

Let us talk about pricing, because many people make the mistake of pricing their product arbitrarily and they end up losing money.

There are many costs you have to factor in to get your last selling price to give you a profit.

Otunba Jide Omiyale – The Dropship Entrepreneur.

The table below will help.

Component	% On Price	Amount
Selling Price		29.99
Cost Of Product	27	7.99
Transaction Fee(Payment Gateway)	3	1.00
Currency Exchange	2	0.60
Shopy Fees	2	0.60
Provision For Returns(8%)	2	0.64
Tax	20	6.0
Shipping Cost	0	0.00
Advert Cost	23	7.00
Other Costs	4	1.15
Total Costs	83	24.94
Profit	17	5.05

NOTE. The above table is hypothetical. You may increase the selling price a bit if you can transfer the increase to the customer. Many customers don't know about those suppliers you are getting your supply from.

In many developing countries, many don't even have the resources like dollar cards to make purchases from the suppliers.

Many dropshippers are making good money from this model.

Tools For Dropshipping.

There are loads of them, and writing about them will take another book. We gave some in the book, but these things change daily. As you progress, you will learn about what to use as your situation demands

Otunba Jide Omiyale – The Dropship Entrepreneur.

Write A Review

To share your experiences, you might choose to write a book review.

In fact, we kindly ask that you write an objective review of the copy of **this book** that you have.

Whether or not you found the books informative, others will value your opinion on them.

Providing an unbiased review of a book can help readers determine whether books are appropriate for them.

Please take the time to go to the book's page on Amazon and write a few words about your thoughts on it.

Scroll down to customers reviews on the left and click the "write a customer review button"

I appreciate you doing this.

About The Author.

Jide Omiyale has a robust MBA foundation, recognized as a business coach and dynamic speaker specializing in empowering small and medium-sized enterprises (SMEs).

With a passion for strategic leadership and sustainable growth, he leverages extensive experience and expertise to inspire actionable insights and drive transformative outcomes for aspiring entrepreneurs.

He is also the author of the following books on Amazon:
- *Profitable Small Business Ideas for Nigeria and Developing Economies.* & *How To Import From China*

www.ingramcontent.com/pod-product-compliance
Lightning Source LLC
Chambersburg PA
CBHW072052230526
45479CB00010B/683